CHICAGO

10737579

RE: CHICAGO
September 17, 2011–March 4, 2012
DePaul Art Museum

© 2011 DePaul University

ISBN 978-0-9789074-3-3

DePaul Art Museum
DePaul University
935 West Fullerton Avenue
Chicago, Illinois 60614

Distributed by the University of Chicago Press
www.press.uchicago.edu

DPAM
DEPAUL ART MUSEUM

TERRA
FOUNDATION FOR AMERICAN ART

This exhibition has been supported in part by a generous grant from the Terra Foundation for American Art.

Cover:
Christina Ramberg, American, 1946–1995
Untitled, c. 1969
Acrylic on pressed board; 11 ½ × 6 in.
Collection of the DePaul Art Museum, Art Acquisition Endowment, 2006.40
© Estate of Christina Ramberg, courtesy of Corbett vs. Dempsey

CONTENTS

FOREWORD 6

ACKNOWLEDGMENTS 9

Wendy Greenhouse — CHICAGO AND THE CANON, PRESENT AND PAST 10

Kirsten M. Jensen — WAS IT REALLY A RUBE TOWN? ART IN CHICAGO BEFORE THE ARMORY SHOW 17

Lynne Warren — LATENT IMAGES: CLAIMING CHICAGO'S EXTRAORDINARY PHOTOGRAPHIC LEGACY 26

Robert Cozzolino — ABJECT POP IN CHICAGO 33

CATALOGUE OF THE EXHIBITION 40

EXHIBITION CHECKLIST 81

NOMINATORS 84

FOREWORD

In 1969 the Museum of Contemporary Art Chicago invited Don Baum, an artist and curator, to organize an exhibition of work by Chicago artists. Baum called his project *Don Baum Says Chicago Needs Famous Artists* and installed works by twenty-eight local artists amidst the ductwork of a large furnace. The gallery space was intended to replicate a domestic basement, down to the wood-grained paneling and bare bulbs dangling from the ceiling. The museum's press release dryly noted that the artists "feel their works will be comfortable here."[1] The installation and its title were ironic, to say the least, but the exhibition gave substance to a significant moment in the long history of shifting and ambivalent relationships between Chicago artists and institutions. Local artists had long felt ignored in favor of those working in New York or Europe, and Baum's show sought to draw awareness to Chicago's neglected art world.

Over forty years later, Baum's premise is still provocative: Who is famous? Who should be? Who used to be? These issues were at the front of our thinking as we began to develop a Chicago-themed exhibition, the first to be displayed in DePaul University's newly constructed museum. Posing these queries to a handful of people in the Chicago art world netted a variety of names, but also some deeper conversations about canonicity—who is in or out and why—and the corollary question of why Chicago artists only become famous if they leave the city. Ultimately, these ideas led to a broader theme: the way in which multiple factors (economic prosperity, political structures, availability of education, and social relations) in a specific locale can engender an imperfectly shared sense of identity, and the way that artists may represent or resist that definition.

What began as informal discussions with colleagues yielded such lively responses that we have tried to incorporate aspects of those exchanges into the theme and structure of the exhibition itself. Rather than selecting works for *Re: Chicago* with a single curatorial eye, we asked about forty individuals involved in the art world—collectors, critics, and scholars—to nominate an artist to our "canon," and we built the exhibition from their responses. Their commentaries on their choices appear in this catalogue, and reading them as a group illuminates several important points. First, our curatorial process deliberately avoided generating a comprehensive list of Chicago artists, or even a coherent one. There are some surprising inclusions and some even more surprising lacunae. Second, the canon is not as fixed as it might seem and depended in large measure on the perspectives of our nominators, many of whom do not normally find themselves in a curatorial role. Third, a significant proportion of the nominees are emerging artists, some of whom have already had impressive success both locally and in the larger art world. Finally, the range of responses, from the scholarly to the intimately personal, is a reminder that reception—how art is seen and understood by viewers—is often as interesting and revelatory as an artist's statement might be. The encounter between object and viewer that is the substance of these commentaries is an important aspect of how reputations are formed. By foregrounding our nominators' responses, we hope that the catalogue and exhibition (where these texts appear on labels) will stimulate conversations, encouraging viewers to form and express their opinions and in so doing expand and destabilize canonical categories.

Arguably, that process of canonical destabilization is already well underway. The past decade has seen several important exhibitions on the topic of art in Chicago, publications on previously obscure artists, and an expansion of Chicago works available in the primary and secondary art markets here and elsewhere. But the project of forming Chicago's historic and contemporary artistic canon remains complex, haunted by implicit and explicit comparisons to the rest of the art world—principally New York and Europe—and a varying degree of anxiety about whether artists should follow trends set elsewhere or carve out their own paths.

The shifting attitudes toward art in Chicago are illuminated by four historical examples discussed by the contributors to this catalogue. Kirsten Jensen probes the industrial expositions of the late nineteenth century, when the prevailing attitudes of Chicago's elite art establishment were informed by the French academic tradition. Two decades later, the Art Institute of Chicago was daring enough to bring the Armory Show to the city, and vast crowds streamed through the galleries during its brief run. As Wendy Greenhouse details, this episode was drastically polarizing, and both the taste for the avant-garde and the reactionary antimodernism it engendered remained potent forces in Chicago for years to come. In the 1930s, it was the former perspective, coupled with an entrepreneurial impulse, that motivated local civic leaders to bring the displaced Bauhaus to Chicago. Lynne Warren explores how that decision set in motion aesthetic and pedagogic practices in photography that still affect how the medium is understood and help to explain why the city's importance as a center for photography is underappreciated. The final essay addresses a distinctive strain in Chicago art that finds full expression in the Hairy Who, six artists whose exhibitions during the late 1960s ignored the hegemonic power of abstraction and reveled in cartoon imagery. In a vitriolic *New York Times* review, John Russell described the participants' work as "repulsive" and linked their aesthetic to the city of Chicago. Yet, Robert Cozzolino suggests, the group had deeper roots and was more closely tied to international Pop Art than has previously been recognized. Indeed, Russell himself acknowledged the artists' expanding influence even as he deplored their methods: "Wherever new art is coarse and tacky in substance . . . and frankly hostile to high art there are likely to be affinities of one kind or another with the Hairy Who."[2] The Hairy Who may mark the moment when Chicago artists began to understand the city as an intellectual and aesthetic asset, not a liability, and position it as a radically oppositional center rather than a peripheral outpost. And if Chicago's artistic past and present are regarded through this lens—another task suggested by our conversations—the distinctiveness and extraordinary character of the place appear as deep imprints on its visual culture.

Even during Chicago's frontier days, prominent citizens were sensitive to the city's reputation of "hustle and muscle," and they were quicker than the residents of many other expanding cities to form educational and cultural institutions. Then as now, the Chicago Academy of Design and its descendant, the Art Institute, provided a venue for both education and social and business exchanges among the wealthy, facilitating the conversion of monetary wealth into social prestige among donors and trustees.

But art also cut across class: in the early twentieth century, numerous schools offered training in graphic and commercial arts, a path to upward mobility via Chicago's vast printing industry. For the disadvantaged and the newly arrived, art in many forms was understood as literally civilizing—a particularly important means of assimilation in a city that in 1900 derived a third of its population from immigration. The Art Institute's education programs; the museum at Hull House, a west-side settlement agency for immigrants; and even private organizations like

Palette and Chisel all grew out of and manifested a faith in the benevolent social effects of art, which now seems at best naive.

Production and consumption of art in Chicago—artists in their studios and collectors in their homes—were a different story, however. Artists faced a tough sell to wealthy clients who wanted the cachet of art bought in Europe or on the East Coast, and institutions like the Art Institute supported local work only erratically. In response, artists formed a remarkable number of exhibition organizations, and sympathetic patrons provided facilities like Tree Studios and the Fine Arts Building. But perhaps for reasons of scale or supply and demand (graduates of the School of the Art Institute and other institutions were abundant), the critical mass of collectors, critics, dealers, artists' hangouts and bars, and other infrastructures of the art world did not coalesce, and artists frequently complained that they had to leave town to earn a reputation—and a living.

Those who remained, and arguably many of those who left, were nevertheless effectively marked by the city, and many artists showed a distinct temperament and set of interests. Chicago style has been parsed repeatedly, and scholars and critics have noted an enduring interest in the human figure, the vernacular aesthetic, and the quality of craftsmanship. All of these characteristics are readily apparent in this exhibition, its group-sourced curatorial perspective notwithstanding. Evident too, although more difficult to pinpoint, is an attitude of truculence, just a step away from confrontation, which is found in, among many others, Ralph Arnold's *Who You/Yeah Baby* (cat. 4), Macena Barton's self-portrait (cat. 5), Morris Topchevsky's *Century of Progress* (cat. 9), and any work from the Hairy Who.

Nevertheless, as this catalogue and the exhibition it accompanies make clear, the term "Chicago artist" remains problematic, and given how elastic the canon of Chicago art has proved to be, so too does the adjective "famous." The formation of reputation depends on the speaker's perspective, on who makes up the critical audience, on connections and opportunities, on technical skill, on the adaptability (or failure) of images and ideas to speak across time, and on a host of other factors seen and unseen. That elusive mutability is at the heart of this project, and we hope that exploring it will initiate new discussions, arguments, and ideas, all appropriate aspirations for a new museum. For in the end, the premise behind Don Baum's exhibition title remains true: Chicago needs, and needs to recognize, its famous artists.

Louise Lincoln
Director, DePaul Art Museum

ENDNOTES

1 News release, "Don Baum Says 'Chicago Needs Famous Artists' Opens at Museum of Contemporary Art," Mar. 3, 1969. Archives, Museum of Contemporary Art, Chicago.

2 John Russell, "Gallery View: 'The Hairy Who' and Other Messages From Chicago," *New York Times*, January 31, 1982.

ACKNOWLEDGMENTS

By its very nature, *Re: Chicago* has drawn on the knowledge and generosity of an unusually broad group of colleagues in the local art world and beyond. Intending to explore different approaches to making and understanding art, we sought out artists and collectors, as well as academics, colleagues in other museums, and those immersed in the history and culture of Chicago. We asked them not only to suggest an artist for inclusion in the exhibition, but also to contribute a commentary about their choice, an unusual task that they carried out with good humor and great perspicacity. A list of our nominators appears on pages 84–85.

We thank the artists whose work fills these pages and the fresh gallery spaces of DePaul's new museum. In numerous instances, they have lent works to the exhibition, and many have made helpful suggestions about the project, thereby demonstrating the comradeship that is one of the hallmarks of the Chicago art world. We are also grateful for the assistance of galleries representing the artists and their estates: Valerie Carberry at Valerie Carberry Gallery; John Corbett and Jim Dempsey at Corbett vs. Dempsey; Stephen Daiter, Michael Welch, and Paul Berlanga at Stephen Daiter Gallery; Julia Fishbach at Kavi Gupta Gallery; Patti Gilford at Patti Gilford Fine Art; Tamsen Greene at Jack Shainman Gallery; Carl Hammer and Yolanda Nieves at Carl Hammer Gallery; Stan Klein at Firecat Gallery; and Monique Meloche at moniquemeloche gallery. We also thank Charles Baum and Maria Baum, Marc Paschke, and Eric Toller.

Private collectors of Chicago art have willingly lent some of their most prized works. We are grateful to Shay and Christopher Brokemond, Mary Green, Barry and Merle Gross, Wayne Miller, Scott Nielson, Michael Owen, and Bob Roth and his assistant, Matthew Dupont.

Other institutions have offered generous support to the project by making works available for loan. We thank in particular Nicole Dizon, director of communications at New Trier Township High School, District 203; Michael Govan, director of the Los Angeles County Museum of Art; Catherine Ricciardelli, registrar at the Terra Foundation for American Art; and David Robertson, director, and Kristina Bottomley, registrar, at the Mary and Leigh Block Museum of Art, Northwestern University. Daniel Schulman offered thoughtful advice, and Janice Dillard, librarian at the Museum of Contemporary Art Chicago, provided valuable research assistance. We are delighted to include in this publication contributions from four scholars: Robert Cozzolino, Wendy Greenhouse, Kirsten Jensen and Lynne Warren.

The DePaul Art Museum staff has juggled the complexities of an ambitious loan exhibition with the disruption and excitement of moving to a new facility. Laura Fatemi managed loans and other registrarial responsibilities with aplomb and designed a remarkably beautiful and effective installation for a diverse and visually complex exhibition. Gregory Harris played an important role in shaping the project and oversaw numerous aspects of the publication and installation. Administrative assistants Geoff Pettys and Alison Kleiman contributed in countless ways, and our valued interns—Dominic Fortunato, Andrea Jones, and Andrew Tripp—brought enthusiasm and a high degree of professionalism to their varied tasks.

Finally, we extend our abiding thanks to the Terra Foundation for American Art—in particular to Elizabeth Glassman, president, and Carrie Haslett, program officer. The foundation's active encouragement of research and exhibitions on American art has had a visible effect on the field, and we are honored to have its support.

Louise Lincoln
Director, DePaul Art Museum

CHICAGO AND THE CANON, PRESENT AND PAST

Wendy Greenhouse

The intellectual construct known as the canon—the roster of "must-haves" that define a field of cultural endeavor—is a self-contradictory creature. Canons are inherently authoritative, premised on notions of enduring, self-evident standards, yet they are equally relative and malleable, subject to continual revision if not deconstruction. Although necessarily used in the singular to describe any particular domain of historical study, "the canon" cannot in practice be solitary or monolithic, for at any moment multiple, if overlapping, assessments of significance, often not consciously articulated, are at play for various constituencies. In art these include not only scholars and curators but also dealers, collectors, and lay consumers of art exhibitions and their spin-off merchandise. By bringing together voices from a variety of such communities, the present exhibition and publication not only highlight a diversity of available agendas and priorities but also promise a creative cacophony from their interaction.

Both the history of the art of Chicago and the wider field of American art have been the products of a lively questioning of the canon. In his 2003 survey of the state of scholarship on American art, John Davis measured the maturation of the field by its development beyond the apologetic or defensive posture that defined it in its formative decades, during the mid-twentieth century, when the more established art-historical world dismissed American art "as kitsch, retrograde, antimodernist, derivative, sentimental, and untheorized"—descriptors that retain a familiar ring for champions of Chicago's homegrown art.[1] As the study of American art has expanded both methodologically and in subject matter, it has not only challenged boundaries of class, gender, race, and geography, but also contested assumptions about the relationships between perceived "centers" of artistic practice (notably New York) and "peripheral" or "regional" settings. Burgeoning attention to Chicago's art history has been the product and beneficiary of such revisionism, even if few individual Chicago artists have made it into recent survey texts, those fraught instruments of canonization.[2]

One telling exception is Archibald J. Motley Jr., now recognized as Chicago's leading visual-arts representative of the national movement for African American cultural self-realization known as the New Negro Movement. Motley enjoyed a promising start as an honored graduate of the School of the Art Institute of Chicago (in 1919) and protégé of its director, subject of a solo exhibition at a New York gallery, and recipient of a Guggenheim Fellowship. For much of his career, however, he was doubly marginalized by his dual status as an African American and a Chicagoan. Only in 1991, a few years after the artist's death, did his paintings reach a wider audience with a traveling retrospective exhibition organized by the Chicago Historical Society (now the Chicago History Museum).[3] That event owed much to the fact that a large proportion of Motley's paintings remained in the hands of one of the museum's curators, who was also the artist's devoted son, as well as to the institution's new commitment to expanding its audience and revising its traditional elitist image. Motley's probing portraits of African Americans and lively Bronzeville scenes seemed

1.1 Archibald J. Motley Jr. (American, 1891–1981). *Nightlife*, 1943. Oil on canvas; 36 × 47 ¾ in. The Art Institute of Chicago, restricted gift of Mr. and Mrs. Marshall Field, Jack and Sandra Guthman, Ben W. Heineman, Ruth Horwich, Lewis and Susan Manilow, Beatrice C. Mayer, Charles A. Meyer, John D. Nichols, and Mr. and Mrs. E.B. Smith, Jr.; James W. Alsdorf Memorial Fund; Goodman Endowment, 1992.89.

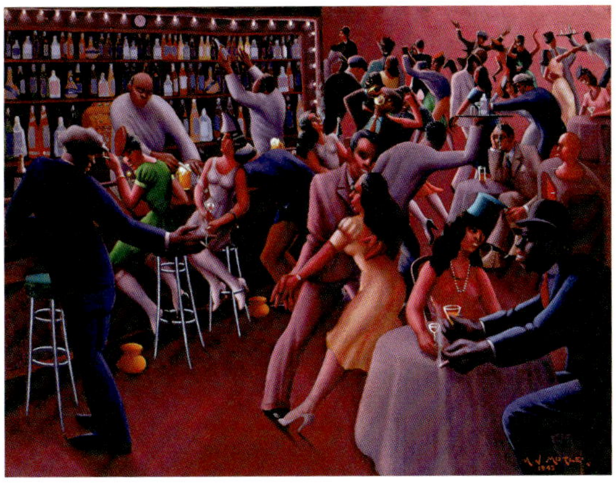

tailor-made for that mission. Deeply rooted in the artist's firsthand observation of manners and mores in the stratified society of black Chicago, his paintings normalized that self-contained world by dignifying it as a subject for artistic treatment.

For a museum devoted to local history, Motley's Chicago association and subject matter were as compelling as his African American identity as reasons to mount a retrospective exhibition of his work, but it was the latter that gained him a place in the broader art-historical canon. In the wake of the exhibition, he became the only artist closely associated with Chicago to be consistently included in surveys of American and twentieth-century American art, beginning with Wayne Craven's *American Art: History and Culture*, published in 1994. Around that time, the Art Institute acquired two Motley paintings, an early self-portrait and one of his signature images of black nightlife (**FIG. I.1**), now one of the museum's more merchandised paintings. Undoubtedly, Motley would be astounded, as well as gratified, at his current canonical status. Yet having resisted categorization as an artist of color at the same time that he resisted exile from his hometown to the art center of New York, he might have found its basis somewhat ironic. Although his acknowledged achievement is rooted in his hometown on multiple levels, as he was the first to recognize, his inclusion in the canon owes much to the racial identity with which he had an intriguingly ambivalent relationship as an artist.

Motley's story is a case study in not just the fluidity of the canon but also the somewhat haphazard nature of its formation. Ultimately, the preservation and wider revelation of his artistic achievement greatly depended on both a particular moment in cultural politics and the fortunate but exceptional coincidence of familial stewardship and institutional connections. The intrinsic merit of Motley's compelling art—which continues to be mined for its engagement with important issues of identity, personification, and the performance of self-presentation—is independent of the kind of contingencies that govern what we know of the art of even the local, not-so-distant past.[4]

Canons are by definition concerned not with what we can know but with what we choose to know. Much of what we have chosen to know of Chicago's artistic past fits into an ongoing process that Davis described as "the contesting and complicating of this narrative of 'the modern' [that] is the drumbeat that drives nearly all of the recent work on early-twentieth-century American art." The visible legacy of Chicago's narrative of the modern certainly contests the canonical modernism defined by the circle of photographer and gallery owner Alfred Stieglitz in New York.[5] As demonstrated by the community of artistic radicals represented by Raymond Jonson, Ramon Shiva, and Rudolph Weisenborn, abstraction and formalism had comparatively little traction among Chicago artists—with the exception of the experimental early paintings of Manierre Dawson (cat. 18). Symbolism, fantasy, and pointed social commentary exerted a pervasive attraction, as the diverse work of artists ranging from Gertrude Abercrombie (cat. 1) to Carl Hoeckner (cat. 22) shows. And Chicago's radicals—several of whom disdained the label "modernist"—shared with their

1.2 Adam Emory Albright (American, 1862–1957). *Cherries Are Ripe*, c. 1903. Oil on canvas; 35 × 74 in. M. Christine Schwartz Collection.

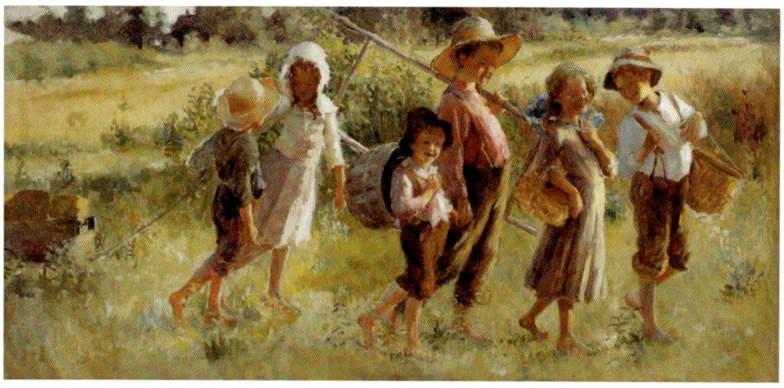

more conservative counterparts an attachment to figuration, meticulous technique, and sheer decorative beauty, albeit sometimes jarringly at odds with pictorial content, all visible in the paintings of Ivan Albright (cat. 2) and Macena Barton (cat. 5).

Chicago's homegrown modernists were united by little more than their very resistance to definition, by the "eccentricity" or "idiosyncrasy" of their art.[6] Indeed, they defined themselves as modernists not so much through their art as through their attitude: an insistence on freedom from establishments, rules, and precedents and a commitment above all to individual self-expression—as manifested by their most characteristic institutional creation, the Chicago No-Jury Society of Artists. While their work may challenge canonical notions of what modernist art looks like, the independence and individuality of their "thinking modern" is far more familiar.

By inviting new ways to define modernism itself, Chicago's modernist artists offered the most compelling claim so far for the city's role in a canonical narrative of American art history. They likewise constitute the emerging canon of early-twentieth-century Chicago art, one that harmonizes with the city's reputation for innovation in architecture and design, city planning, and the literary arts, as well as adventurous private collecting and exhibiting. In this flattering narrative of the triumph of modernism, the "old guard" of more conservative artists who formed the leadership of Chicago's early-twentieth-century art establishment is conspicuously sidelined. The contemporary prominence and popular success of the likes of Adam Emory Albright, Pauline Palmer, Frank Peyraud, and Lorado Taft, for example, testify to Chicago's conservative fine-art temperament even as they provide a convenient foil for modernism in the narrative of its ascent. In contrast to the once-marginalized Motley, these artists were the ultimate insiders in the art community of Chicago in their day, the principal representatives of and leading influences within a vast, now-submerged world of creative practice and prestige that survives only in records of press coverage, organizational activity, patronage, and similar public measures of contemporary importance. Notwithstanding the evolution of the canon, they remain irrefutably if inconveniently present—not merely as a backdrop for modernist rebellion but also as the center of the full narrative of Chicago's art history between the 1893 World's Columbian Exposition and the Great Depression. The local canon of that era, in which they loomed large, stubbornly persists as an index of their historical importance—and of the role of the canon-envy that has deeply shaped both the city's art history and posterity's perceptions of it.

If Chicago's modernists can be defined by their individuality, its mainstream artists are remarkable for their conformity—not so much in artistic style as in a shared conviction of uplift as art's highest function and beauty as its medium. In this they aptly expressed their upstart city's anxieties about its position on the cultural periphery. In its officially sanctioned art, "Chicago, perhaps just because it knows that the world is likely to accuse it of the contrary, is, if anything, almost unduly anxious to be modest, quiet, and

1.3 Frank C. Peyraud (Swiss, 1858–1948). *After Rain, Chicago*, 1911. Oil on canvas; 36 ½ × 46 ⅛ in. The Art Institute of Chicago, Friends of American Art Collection, 1913.133.

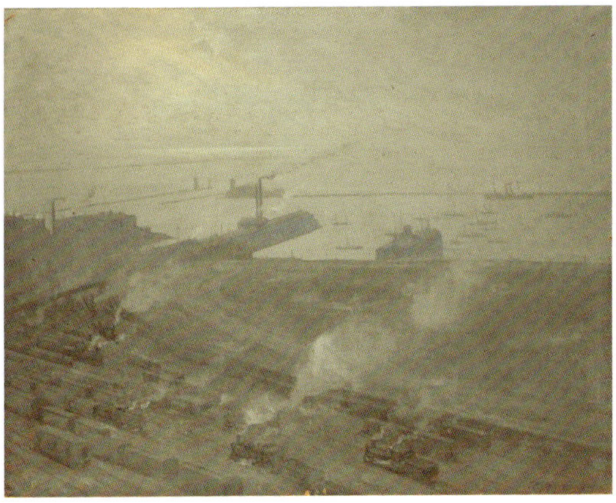

well-bred," *Harper's Magazine* observed in 1917.[7] Its mainstream art was one of accessibility and comfort, of "sanity" and "good taste," that "reflects the nobler side of daily living . . . shows aspiration for fairer things and is true to nature."[8]

Its deliberate repudiation of ugliness and impermanence is epitomized in Adam Albright's enormously popular Impressionist paintings of carefree rural children, which, according to approving reviewers, offered a therapeutic dose of nostalgia for many a harried Chicago businessman with memories of a bucolic boyhood (see **FIG. 1.2**).[9] Such artful euphemism came into play most effectively in picturing Chicago itself. A bold encounter with one of the city's grittier prospects, the railroad yards blanketing the industrial lakefront, could be, as in Peyraud's *After Rain, Chicago* (**FIG. 1.3**), a "poetic interpretation" in which "the mists and smoke veil and soften the harsher realities." Proof that a true artist's eye could find "beauty and picturesque subject matter" even in Chicago, this prizewinner in the Art Institute's 1913 *Chicago and Vicinity* annual exhibition was purchased for the museum by the Friends of American Art.[10] Nothing more closely referenced Chicago than the effort to transcend the visual and spiritual shortcomings of what writer Hamlin Garland succinctly described as a "drab expanse of desolate materialism" or to reconcile such a setting with canonical values.[11] That project was deeply inflected by the city's uncomfortable relationship with the canon and its anxiety for inclusion—a defining theme in Chicago's history that resonates in the animating premise of the present publication.

Perhaps no Chicago artist was more directly concerned with the city's status as a cultural outsider than Lorado Taft. Equipped with the necessary prestige of training at Paris's École des Beaux-Arts, he launched his career in Chicago, in the late 1880s, just as public sculpture came into its heyday as a respected expression of cultural authority. Chicago's most celebrated and productive public artist from the 1890s through the 1930s, he was equally prominent as a self-appointed missionary for art, darling of the lecture circuit, prolific writer, and beloved educator. Taft remains the most articulate spokesman for the lofty art ideals of his generation in Chicago and its ambition to apply them both to the expression of the city's aspirations and to the amelioration of its abundant ills. Chicago, noted Taft, had not only to "build a reputation but we have got to overcome one . . . we have got to show them something more than our stock yards, our miles of railways, our great commercial enterprises, we have got to show them there is a spirit behind it all which has its ideals of another character."[12]

If Motley emblematizes the restoration of the mistakenly marginalized, Taft exemplifies the fall into anti-canonical status of the formerly renowned. While such lights as Adam Albright and Peyraud quietly faded from prominence before their deaths around mid-century, the "lecturing taxidermist" was transmuted into a lasting target for modernist derision, an image that has long overshadowed his once-towering status as Chicago's most distinguished artist.[13] Locally, Taft may be known as the creator of such familiar monuments as the mammoth statue of Blackhawk, near Oregon,

1.4 Lorado Taft (American, 1860–1936). *Fountain of the Great Lakes* (1913), in its original location on the south side of the Art Institute of Chicago. n.d. Lorado Taft Papers, University of Illinois Archives.

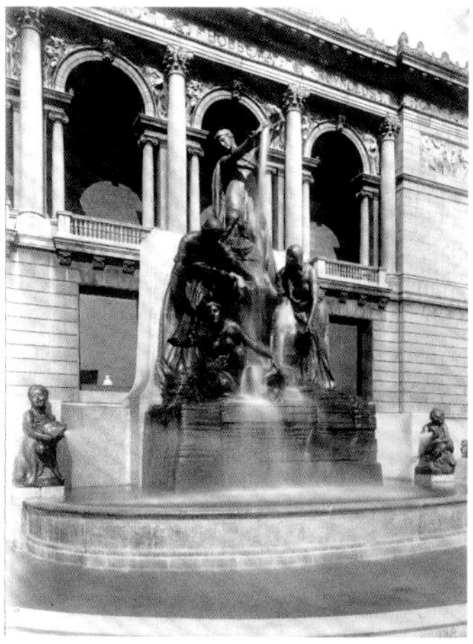

1.5 Lorado Taft (American, 1860–1936). *The Solitude of the Soul*, modeled in plaster, 1901; sculpted in marble, 1914. Marble; h. 91 in.; base 51 × 41 ½ in. The Art Institute of Chicago, Friends of American Art Collection, 1914.739.

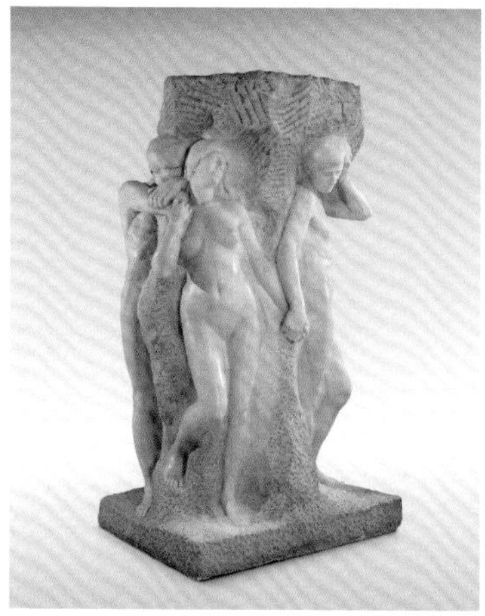

Illinois, and the *Fountain of Time* on Chicago's Midway, the recent restoration of which signals a quiet resurgence of respect for the artist. For decades, however, his wider renown largely rested on the longevity of his pioneering 1903 *History of American Sculpture* (reissued for decades, it remains available as a print-on-demand book). In it he traced the progressive development of an American sculpture tradition as the foundation for the many contemporary practitioners who fill the second half of the text. "What was at first the mere groping of an untaught instinct, destitute of message or appeal, has gradually developed a character, a fundamental sincerity, and remarkable gifts of utterance," he concluded hopefully. In chronicling a succession of practitioners, the text offers the assurance of lineage for what Taft proclaimed a vital national art, if one still laboring under a sense of exclusion from the canon. His text both champions a new, native canon and makes a case for its worthiness in the judgment of art history. In this respect, it mirrors his identity as a Chicago artist.

Notwithstanding the modernists' charge of "canonizing the past," Taft subscribed to the Progressive Era–notion of a usable history, a dynamic source of inspiration and guidance for the future. In the eventual evolution of his own sculptural work, he served, as Allen Weller noted, as a "bridge, though an unwilling one" between Beaux-Arts tradition and the new art of the 1930s.[14]

The American artist, Taft argued in the conclusion of his *History of American Sculpture*, "must speak no alien tongue, but must follow the vernacular of his day and race," yet do so through an accommodation with traditional artistic values.[15] His *Fountain of the Great Lakes* (**FIG. 1.4**), completed in 1913 as the first commission from the Ferguson Fund for the beautification of Chicago through public monuments, demonstrated his notion of a synthesis of local and ideal, modern and canonically sanctioned, using a restrained Beaux-Arts classicism to elevate indigenous subject matter. The work tied the region's outstanding natural feature to a heroic narrative of "nature's metropolis," the city that owed its existence to its lakeside location at the geographical heart of the nation's commerce. Taft's fountain also linked the past to the future: its very conventionality of expression and inoffensive blandness were a hopeful statement about Chicago's immanence as a center of high culture, an assertion of the city's ambition to join the great tradition represented by the canonical artists whose names were enshrined directly above the fountain, on the cornice of the Art Institute's exterior walls. The challenge of melding the timeless and the local can be measured in the bifurcated criticism of Taft's fountain: its decorous ladies scandalized some viewers with their seminudity, while disappointing others as inappropriately tame representations of the lakes' tumultuous waters.

Where his fountain celebrated Chicago, Taft's *The Solitude of the Soul* (**FIG. 1.5**) used a similar formal language of idealized figuration to obliquely critique the urban existence it epitomized, to remedy Chicago's lamentable lack of the "traditions" that "give us greater solidarity," "put a soul into our community," and "make us love this place above all others."[16] Apparently neither prompted by a commission nor inspired by any text, *The Solitude of the Soul* evolved from a 1901 plaster model to the monumental carved marble completed in 1914 for the Art Institute. Its four figures, linked by touch but ultimately blind to one another, embody existential loneliness—a universal condition with obvious implications for Chicago as a symbol of the anomie of contemporary urban existence.[17] Taft redeemed the pessimism of this theme through the very act of giving it sculptural expression, thereby reifying his ideal of art as an agent of civic community through cultural consensus; the artist may even have imagined the sculpture creating a kind of spontaneous community of viewers, who circle it to observe it from all sides.

Taft's work represents a singular moment in Chicago's cultural development, when the sculptor and his fellow members of the artistic establishment imagined the city poised to not only join but also redefine the canon, directing its evolution toward an authentically American expression. Its natural and inevitable source, they projected wishfully, was rightfully the "fresh, virile, independent civilization of the great plains," with Chicago as its capital.[18] Taft was evidently galvanized by the challenge of bringing Chicago up to the standard of the canon by applying its values to expressing and remediating the city. By startling coincidence, both the dedication of the *Fountain of the Great Lakes* and the completion of the marble rendering of *The Solitude of the Soul* occurred within the same year that the Art Institute hosted the notorious Armory Show. The traveling exhibition of contemporary modernist art signaled the advent of new art idioms that ultimately eclipsed both the artistic old guard and the moral and expressive values it upheld. Ironically, the ideals of continuity, community, and the timeless expression of abstract universals in which Taft placed his faith proved far more transient than the modernist paradigms of iconoclasm and individual self-expression. As artists, with increasing confidence, sourced their own validity, their attitude of independence from the canon came to define its ongoing evolution—and Chicago's bid for admission into it. In the formation of a canon of Chicago's historical artists, the question of the city's relationship to outside artistic authority remains doggedly persistent.

ENDNOTES

1 John Davis, "The End of the American Century: Current Scholarship on the Art of the United States," *Art Bulletin* 85 (Sept. 2003): 561.

2 See, for example, Frances Pohl, *Framing America: A Social History of American Art*, 2nd ed. (New York: Thames & Hudson, Inc., 2008); and Angela L. Miller et al., *American Encounters: Art, History, and Cultural Identity* (Upper Saddle River, NJ: Pearson Education, Inc., 2008).

3 See Jontyle Theresa Robinson and Wendy Greenhouse, *The Art of Archibald J. Motley, Jr.* (Chicago: Chicago Historical Society, 1991).

4 On the identity politics and social function of Motley's portraits, see Amy M. Mooney, *Archibald J. Motley Jr.* (San Francisco: Pomegranate Communications, Inc., 2004); Phoebe Wolfskill, "Caricature and the New Negro in the Work of Archibald Motley Jr. and Palmer Hayden," *Art Bulletin* 41 (Sept. 2009): 341–65; and Mooney's forthcoming book *Portraits of Noteworthy Character*.

5 See Susan Weininger, "'The Spirit of Change': Modernism in Chicago," in Wendy Greenhouse and Susan Weininger, *Chicago Painting, 1895 to 1945: The Bridges Collection* (Urbana/Springfield: University of Illinois Press/Illinois State Museum, 2004), 56–59.

6 Robert Cozzolino, "Chicago's Modernism," in *Art in Chicago: Resisting Regionalism, Transforming Modernism* (Philadelphia: Pennsylvania Academy of the Fine Arts, 2007), 13–18; Susan Weininger, "Fantasy in Chicago Painting: 'Real "Crazy," Real Personal, and Real Real,'" in Elizabeth Kennedy et al., *Chicago Modern, 1893–1945: Pursuit of the New* (Chicago: Terra Museum of American Art/Terra Foundation for the Arts, 2004), 67.

7 Harrison Rhodes, "The Portrait of Chicago," *Harper's Magazine* 135 (June 1917): 89.

8 Untitled clipping from *Chicago Post*, Oct. 31, 1908, scrapbooks, vol. 24, The Art Institute of Chicago.

9 G. D. B., "Art and Artists," *Chicago Journal*, Oct. 13, 1900.

10 Minnie Bacon Stevenson, "By the Lake—Chicago," *The Art Student* 1 (1913): 114.

11 Hamlin Garland, *Daughter of the Middle Border*, quoted in Lewis Waldron Williams, "Lorado Taft: American Sculptor and Art Missionary" (PhD diss., University of Chicago, 1958), 69.

12 Taft, quoted in "Ways and Means Committee Exhibits Association's Gift to Boston and Takes Inspiring Counsel on Spirit and Uses of Civic Art," *Chicago Commerce*, May 17, 1912, Taft Papers, box 18, University of Illinois Urbana-Champaign Archives.

13 Allen Weller, "Lorado Taft, the Ferguson Fund, and the Advent of Modernism," in Sue Ann Prince, ed., *The Old Guard and the Avant-Garde: Modernism in Chicago, 1910–1940* (Chicago: University of Chicago Press, 1990), 39. On Taft's role as an art missionary to Chicago, see Timothy J. Garvey, *Public Sculptor: Lorado Taft and the Beautification of Chicago* (Urbana: University of Illinois Press, 1988).

14 Weller (note 13), 57.

15 Lorado Taft, *History of American Sculpture* (New York/London: Macmillan Company, 1903), 537.

16 Lorado Taft, "The Fountain of the Great Lakes: Its Origin and Meaning Told by Its Sculptor, Lorado Taft," clipping from unidentified newspaper, Oct. 9, 1913, Taft Papers, box 23, University of Illinois Urbana-Champaign Archives.

17 Judith Barter et al., *American Arts at the Art Institute of Chicago: From Colonial Times to World War I* (Chicago: Art Institute of Chicago, 1998), 286.

18 H. F. Kuehne, "Lorado Taft, Sculptor of the West," *Austin American*, Apr. 5, 1915, Taft Papers, box 23, University of Illinois Urbana-Champaign Archives.

WAS IT REALLY A RUBE TOWN?

ART IN CHICAGO BEFORE THE ARMORY SHOW

Kirsten M. Jensen

Over the century that now separates us from the 1913 Armory Show, the groundbreaking exhibition has come to be remembered as an extravagant, flamboyant spectacle, one that has colored our perception of Chicago's cultural development. Many Chicagoans responded skeptically to the modern art featured in the Armory Show. While it was on view at the Art Institute of Chicago, teachers complained of young girls gazing at "distorted art," critics decried the "lewd" and "demoralizing" pictures, and art students found "Hennery O'Hair Mattress" (Matisse) guilty of "artistic murder, pictorial arson, [and] total degeneracy of color sense" and condemned him to death (see **FIG. 2.1**).[1] Indeed, today many believe Armory Show organizer Walt Kuhn's infamous statement that Chicago was "a rube town."[2] Over the years, others have added to this dialogue, most notably Milton Brown, who wrote in his history of the Armory Show, "[Chicago] was not only more provincial, but it suffered from a badly concealed sense of inferiority [to New York]."[3] Such an understanding of Chicago as a cultural backwater with an inferiority complex—one unable to appreciate modern art—corresponds well to the nicknames that have been lobbed at it by rivals throughout history: "Porkopolis" or "The Windy City" (both bequeathed by Cincinnati), which suggest Chicago is all bombast and no substance. But this narrow view overlooks the long history of art and cultural development in the city, particularly between 1880 and 1913, which suggests a more complex, and certainly more sophisticated, approach to the kind of modernism the Armory Show presented. This is a history that, in light of the goals presented by *Re: Chicago*, deserves a closer look.

Our impression of art in Chicago at the turn of the century is bracketed by the great display of Impressionist art at the 1893 World's Columbian Exposition and the Armory Show, with little knowledge of what came before or what went on in the twenty years that separated these influential displays. Almost from Chicago's founding in 1837, art was a centerpiece of the city's cultural life, and the first public exhibition was held in 1859.[4] Arts organizations, patrons, critics, and the public demonstrated an early interest in European art, as well as art by Americans who had worked abroad. Chicagoans prided themselves on the fact that the same pioneering and adventurous spirit that pervaded their civic viewpoint was projected onto their artistic endeavors. To be sure, many of these early efforts were organized with a "we will show them" attitude that attempted to counter dismissive views on the East Coast toward the western upstart.

Most significant of these early artistic activities was the establishment of the Art Gallery at the annual Interstate Industrial Exposition (1873–90) (see **FIG. 2.2**).[5] The exposition's organizers had not originally intended to include art in their fair, but recognized that it could be used as a way of demonstrating Chicago's cultural, as well as industrial, development. Subsequently, they explicitly designed a gallery and annual exhibition intended to rival, and even surpass, what could be seen in New York. They constructed an enormous exhibition space with fifteen thousand linear feet, and they set out to select the best and most

2.1 On April 16, 1913, the closing day of the Armory Show, students of the School of the Art Institute assembled outside the museum to protest the exhibition. The gathering staged a mock trial of Henri Matisse and burned copies of three of his paintings. Archives, The Art Institute of Chicago.

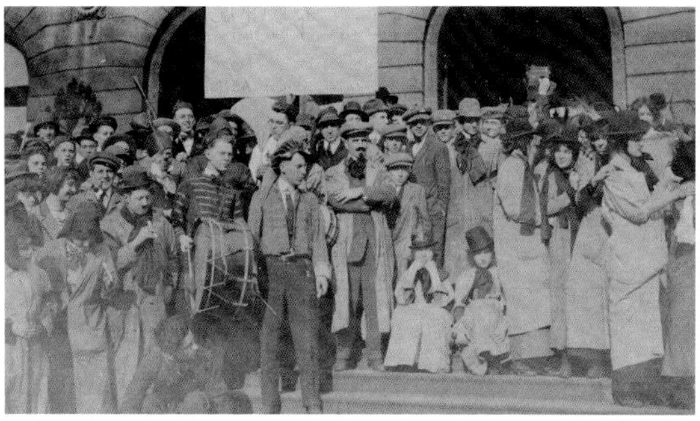

2.2 Photographer unknown. *Interstate Exposition Building, Main View of Building and Grounds*, 1874. Chicago History Museum, ICHi-02170.

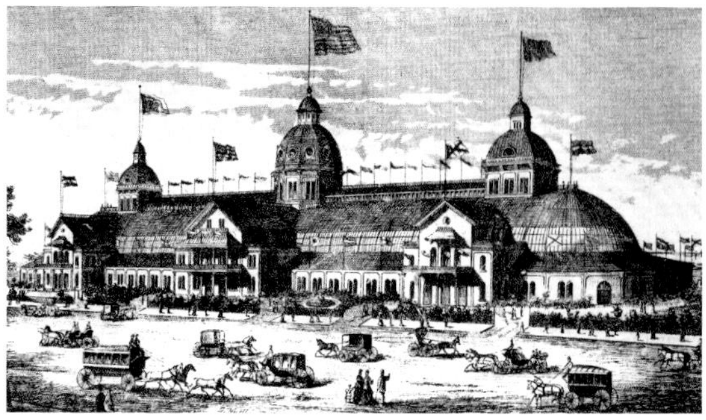

representative works of the newest and most progressive trends in American art.

Initially, the exhibitions that took place at this gallery were peripheral to those occurring in New York, and their organizers took whatever they could get from artists and dealers there (in true Chicago fashion, they offered free shipping as an inducement). But in 1880 the situation changed with the hiring of Sara T. Hallowell, an American who divided her time between Paris and Chicago, to oversee the art gallery.[6] Under Hallowell's direction, it became thoroughly cosmopolitan, with a decidedly Parisian character. She selected paintings and sculpture from the walls of the Salon and artists' studios, and then sent them directly to Chicago, usually bypassing New York on the way. For the first time, Chicago had its own cultural "exclusive." One newspaper remarked:

> Usually the year succeeding the French [Salon] is enough to satisfy the ordinary American as to the merits of some few pictures that remain unsold and drift over the ocean in search of a buyer. Chicago wants them when they are novelties, while hot from France with a halo of sensation about them, and the exhalations of laudation, and she gets them (see **FIG. 2.3**).[7]

By 1885 Chicago had earned an international reputation for its progressive civic character, cosmopolitanism, and annual art exhibition, which was lauded for its liberal policies—qualities that led the *Magazine of Art* to warn the leading art centers of the East to "look to [their] laurels, if [they] would not be entirely outdone" by Chicago.[8]

Chicago's growing confidence in its identity as a national cultural center was further bolstered by the exhibition of eighteen works by French Impressionists at the Art Gallery in 1890—the largest group exhibition of Impressionism in the United States since an 1886 show at the New York gallery of Paul Durand-Ruel. This triumph came at a time when the city was engaged in a heated battle with New York to host the World's Columbian Exposition, which it won—much to the surprise of everyone but those who knew Chicago could fortify its claims with more than just money. If any sense of inferiority in relation to New York remained among its populace at that point, it disappeared in the face of the splendor and cosmopolitan character of the White City of the World's Columbian Exposition—to some it was truly as if Paris had landed on the shores of Lake Michigan.

Perhaps Chicago's new status as a cultural capital was as much a hindrance as it was a benefit—the White City put Chicago on the cultural map, but it proved a hard act to follow, particularly as the culture it codified became increasingly perceived as old-fashioned. Still the ambition that had fueled the city's efforts to raise its profile and the pride that it had attained that goal continued to be a guiding force at the Art Institute of Chicago, which sought to keep its audience "constantly informed of current achievement and thought in the world."[9] This mission assumed that Chicago had established itself and that the character of its reputation was grounded in its willingness to show modern and emerging art styles. As were most academic exhibitions prior to 1913, the museum's

2.3 Alexander Harrison (American, 1853–1930). *Bord du mer (Children on the Beach)*, n.d. Oil on canvas; 60 × 45 in. San Antonio Art League and Museum. *Bord du mer* received an honorable mention at the Salon of 1885. Sara Hallowell selected it from the Salon for the Art Gallery at the Chicago Interstate Exposition that autumn.

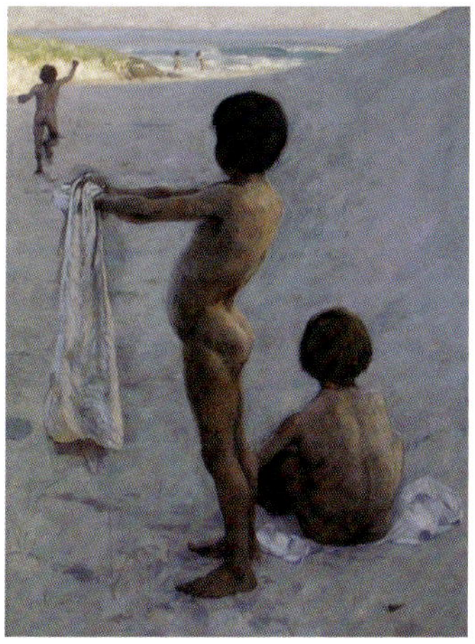

annual American shows were pleasant and boring, but efforts were made to "enlarge" its range through an array of temporary exhibitions that showcased more controversial works of art.[10]

There were, of course, regular exhibitions of Impressionists, both American (such as William Merritt Chase, Maurice Prendergast, and John Twachtman) and European (including Édouard Manet, Claude Monet, and Fritz Thaulow), which fed the city's seemingly endless appetite for the style, but there were also exhibitions that explored more contemporary movements, such as one in 1907 featuring German painting, including the works of Symbolists like Franz von Stuck. In organizing the show, William M. R. French, the director of the Art Institute, voiced reservations about including Von Stuck's overtly sexual paintings *Salome* and *Saheret*, which the museum's president, Charles Hutchinson, had found disagreeable. But the paintings were featured in the exhibition despite these concerns.[11] In 1908 French also made an attempt to organize an exhibition of the work of German Expressionist Emile Nolde, although plans for the show were later shelved due to burdensome importation fees.[12]

That September the Art Institute firmly established itself as a progressive organization in the eyes of American artists when it opened its galleries to the "men of rebellion" and "apostles of ugliness"—otherwise known as The Eight—whose landmark exhibition at Macbeth Gallery in New York several months earlier had caused an uproar. French supported his decision to show The Eight in a museum setting in a letter to Halsey Ives, the director of the Saint Louis City Museum (St. Louis Art Museum), arguing that the group's work should be seen, even if only for its educational value, a position that governed his stance on modern art generally during the remainder of his lengthy tenure at the Art Institute.[13] The significance of the museum setting for an exhibition of artists who were rebelling against the New York art establishment cannot be understated. French's somewhat ambiguous argument about showing The Eight notwithstanding, Chicago essentially placed itself firmly in support of American modernism with this exhibition—a position no New York museum was willing to assume.

At the turn of the twentieth century, Chicago was recognized as a national leader and innovator in architecture, literature, and civic planning, but many of its artists were also pioneering. In a 1908 address to the Arche Club, a group devoted to supporting the arts, sculptor Lorado Taft remarked:

> Chicago is at this moment a greater art center than New York. New York has more artists, but Chicago has better artists because they are fresher and more original. . . . Chicago artists strike out for themselves and create new lines. . . . One reason for our advancement is your great enthusiasm.[14]

The generally progressive attitude that governed the exhibition program at the Art Institute and the subsequent support of the museum-going public drew like-minded artists to the city. Among those who lived in Chicago were Swedish-born B. J. O. Nordfeldt (1878–1955), who, in addition to painting, worked as a set designer for the radical

2.4 B. J. O. Nordfeldt (American, born Sweden, 1878–1955). *Fisherman's Family*, 1916. Woodcut on paper; 12 × 11 in. Amon Carter Museum of American Art, Fort Worth, Texas, 1987.82.

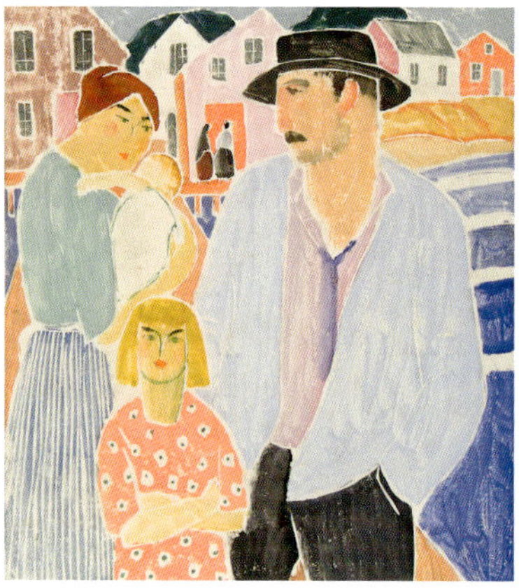

2.5 Frank Lloyd Wright (American, 1867–1959). Thurber Art Gallery, Chicago, 1909. Collection of the Frank Lloyd Wright Preservation Trust.

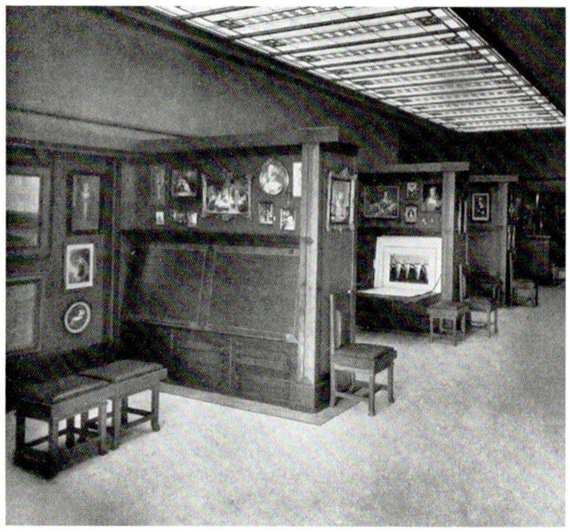

Little Theater; the Fauve Jerome Blum (1884–1956), who had exhibited at the Salon d'Automne in Paris in 1909 and 1910; and the largely self-taught Manierre Dawson (1887–1969), who worked in a nonobjective style (see **FIG. 2.4**, cat. 18). All three were among the first American artists to incorporate into their work the formalist elements traditionally associated with the European avant-garde.

Both Blum and Nordfeldt exhibited at the W. Scott Thurber Gallery (in 1911 and 1912, respectively)—Chicago's most progressive gallery at the time—located on Michigan Avenue adjacent to the Auditorium Building (in what is now known as the Fine Arts Building). In 1909 the gallery was renovated by Frank Lloyd Wright to create a modern interior that was suitable to display modern art, much like Alfred Stieglitz's Gallery 291 in New York (see **FIG. 2.5**). This made it the ideal setting for an exhibition of paintings and pastels by Arthur Dove (1880–1946), who was a member of Stieglitz's circle. Dove's show, considered the first exhibition of abstract art by an American, came to Chicago directly from Stieglitz's gallery in March 1912,[15] and its primary focus was a group of ten abstract pastels, now referred to as the "Ten Commandments" (**FIG. 2.6**). Reviews by local art critics, although generally skeptical of the viability of abstract art as the "art of the future," were largely serious and analytical in their approach to Dove's "absolutist" view of nature.[16] Indeed, the critical reception of the exhibition in Chicago was far better than what had appeared in the New York press.[17] New York critics had been intrigued by Dove's abstractions, but they offered little insight into his aims; Chicago critics, on the other hand, appeared to have made an effort to speak to the artist and to understand his intentions. They may not have agreed with the validity of his nonrepresentational works, but generally they were open to discussing them. Critic George Cram Cook remarked, "Anyone with eyes can see the new energy [in Dove's work]—breaking away into the untried, experimenting, taking new hold of visual elements."[18]

Perhaps encouraged by the exhibitions of modern art at Thurber's gallery, the Art Institute began to investigate the possibility of exhibitions that were more daring than anything it had yet organized. In February 1912, French wrote to Hallowell:

> It has crossed my mind that a small collection of works by the post-impressionists or Cubists might be found interesting here. . . . We have always been willing to give audiences heresies and advanced ideas. . . . There is much curiosity with regard to these works here, and we have never seen anything but reproductions.[19]

Hallowell, who had been the first art agent to attempt to sell paintings by Paul Cézanne in the United States,[20] was certainly up to the task, though she never organized a Cubist show for the museum. In any event, Chicago did not have to wait long. The following year, the Art Institute provided three opportunities for audiences to see the "heresies and advanced ideas" making waves in Europe: the exhibitions *Contemporary German Graphic Art* in January; *Contemporary Scandinavian*

2.6 Arthur Dove (American, 1880–1946). *Nature Symbolized No. 2*, c. 1911. Pastel on paper; 18 × 22 ½ in. The Art Institute of Chicago, Alfred Stieglitz Collection, 1949.533.

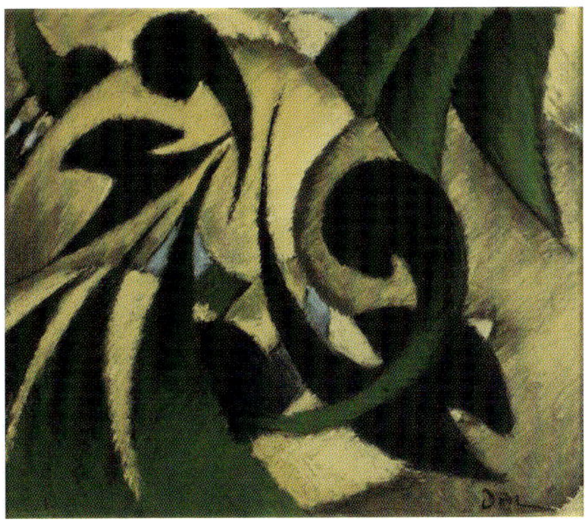

2.7 Jens Ferdinand Willumsen (Danish, 1863–1958). *The Painter and His Family*, 1912. Oil on canvas; 90 × 95 in. J. F. Willumsens Museum, Denmark.

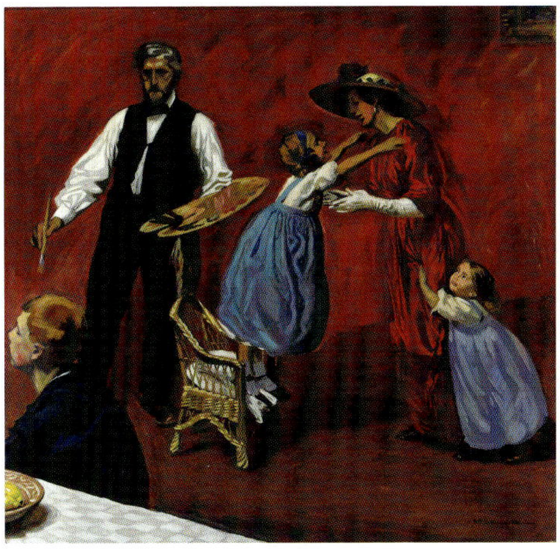

Art, organized by the American-Scandinavian Foundation in New York, from mid-February to mid-March; and, for three weeks in late March and early April, the International Exhibition of Modern Art, otherwise known as the Armory Show. These displays contained art that was far more radical than anything Chicago audiences had seen up to that point (with the exception of exhibitions at the Thurber Gallery), and the varying responses to them suggest that, despite all the sensational publicity that surrounded the Armory Show, the public had a real desire to both see and understand the art of the new.

The German exhibition held at the Art Institute included prints and drawings by leading artists of the Austrian and German avant-garde: Max Beckmann, Lovis Corinth, American-born Lyonel Feininger, Vassily Kandinsky, Käthe Kollwitz, Wilhelm Lehmbruck, Franz Marc, Emile Nolde, and Max Pechstein. The show passed without much press, but what was printed reflected an engaged curiosity as well as a desire to understand the artists' aesthetic motivation. The most caustic—yet dead-on—criticism was Maude Oliver's declaration that the works in the exhibition demonstrated "an avowed anti-perspective performance."[21]

The same could not be said for the Scandinavian exhibition, however. Many local critics lashed out at the works on display, which included paintings by Edvard Munch and his fellow Norwegians Ludvig Karsten, Per Krohg, Henrik Lund, and Oluf Wold-Torne, as well as the Danish painters Harald Giersing, Sigurd Swane, Edvard Weihe, and Jens Ferdinand Willumsen, who had been an associate of Paul Gauguin's in Pont-Aven. All of these artists participated in the Parisian scene, and many were members of the most progressive movements in their own countries, such as the Danish group Den Frie Udstilling (Free Exhibition), which had similar aims to the Salon d'Autumne in Paris. Critics misidentified them as "Futurists" and pronounced their paintings "weird . . . absolutely lacking in everything that is usually associated with the original conceptions in art; hideous delineations which look as if they were conceived in a nightmare and executed in a delirium."[22] About Willumsen's Gauguin-esque painting *The Painter and His Family* (**FIG. 2.7**), George B. Zug remarked, "I neither profess to understand why he cared to paint [it], much more send it over to scream at us who have done nothing to hurt him."[23] One painting was removed from the show on moral grounds, though its removal was almost universally decried in the press—even by those who were rather less than favorably inclined toward much of the exhibition.[24]

Historians have commented on Chicago's "lack of sophistication about modern art and the apprehension that many felt toward it,"[25] as suggested by the scandals surrounding the Scandinavian exhibition, but they tend to overlook the many thoughtful and sophisticated responses to the art expressed in the press. Most critics acknowledged that the exhibition was significant for the further development of art in Chicago; even Zug was forced to admit, "Whether we like the exhibition now at the Art Institute or not, it is bound to stimulate discussion and to enlighten us."[26] And Chicago's citizens lined up to be enlightened. In four days, the Art Institute sold five hundred exhibition catalogues at sixty cents apiece, and attendance reached thirteen thousand on a single day.[27] Members of the local American-Scandinavian Society took visitors on tours of the galleries and explained the principles behind pictures like Willumsen's *The Painter and His Family*. French noted in a letter written shortly after the exhibition opened, the "Scandinavian exhibition proves of great importance and is very successful. I suspect that it does not represent the more conservative painters of Scandinavia . . . [but it] is rather a good stepping stone to the Post-Impressionists [in the Armory Show]."[28]

In the main, there was very little difference between the content of the German and Scandinavian exhibitions, but the latter had the misfortune to open at the Art Institute at the same time the Armory Show was opening in New York. Chicago critics took their cue from the New York press, which focused on the sensational aspects of the Armory Show, and subsequently whipped themselves into a frenzy—mostly on grounds of morality rather than aesthetics.[29] Chicago's response to the Armory Show has been well-documented elsewhere, but what generally receives little attention is that most of the excitement surrounding the exhibition came in the weeks leading up to it—that is, while it was still in New York, where the press was holding its own three-ring circus.[30] It was during this period that Kuhn made his now-famous remark about Chicagoans as unsophisticated rubes. And it was at this point—after more than three decades of relatively liberal-minded exhibition policies and a willing embrace of the new in both European and American art—that a sense of inferiority began to creep back into Chicago's cultural cosmology. It is that feeling of inadequacy—embarrassment, even—that continues to inform our understanding of the city's early-twentieth-century culture. Chicago's response to modern art was a mixed bag, to be sure. However, it must be said that in Chicago, modern art, in its many variations, regularly had something that no other city in the United States was willing to give it before 1913: the opportunity to be seen in a creditable and established cultural venue. As director of the Art Institute, French admitted he was old-fashioned, "heretical" even, but he did not intend to let that prevent others from seeing modern art at the museum so that they could make up their own minds concerning its merits.

In fact, after a few weeks in town, even Kuhn changed his tune. Once the Armory Show opened, more rational voices and balanced views prevailed. Harriet Monroe wrote articles begging for a "fair play" for modern art.[31] There were so many questions about the Post-Impressionists that the Chicago subcommittee for the American Association of Painters and Sculptors issued a pamphlet, edited by Frederick J. Gregg and titled *For and Against*, that presented both favorable and unfavorable opinions about the art on display. Like the exhibition catalogue, it quickly sold out and had to be reprinted. The Art Institute offered lectures giving opinions on both sides of the debate over the validity of modern art—by Charles Francis Brown (against) and Arthur Jerome Eddy (for)—for which "the crush was so great that the Hall could have been filled three or four times."

The Chicago Fortnightly Club, a women's organization, also sponsored several discussions about modern art. By the end of the exhibition's three-week run, nearly 200,000 people had crammed into the galleries to see the twentieth-century version of the latest, greatest, and best.[32] Kuhn later wrote to Elmer MacRae, who was in town to pack up the show, "[Please] tell everybody in Chicago (I mean this) that I had a glorious time."[33] Chicago, it turns out, was not such a rube town after all.

ENDNOTES

1 For the teacher's claims, see "May Bar Youngsters from Cubist's Show," *Chicago Record-Herald*, Mar. 27, 1913. See also "Futurist Art Included in State Vice Inquiry," *Chicago Daily Journal*, Apr. 1, 1913; "Cubist Art Exhibit Ends at Stake," *Chicago Record-Herald*, Apr. 17, 1913; and "Students Wreak Vengeance upon Cubist Designs," *Chicago Evening Post*, Apr. 17, 1913. The students originally intended to burn Matisse in effigy; Walter Pach and Elmer MacRae, the representatives for the Association of American Painters and Sculptors, and the Art Institute's Newton Carpenter interceded, and student copies of *Le Luxe*, *Goldfish and Sculpture*, and *Blue Nude* were burned instead.

2 Walter Kuhn to Elmer MacRae, Apr. 14, 1913, Elmer MacRae/Armory Show Papers, Hirshhorn Museum and Sculpture Garden, Smithsonian Institution.

3 Milton Brown, *The Story of the Armory Show* (Greenwich: New York Graphic Society, 1963), 196.

4 The city's first public art exhibition was held in an iron-clad building known as Burch's Block, located on the corner of Lake Street and Wabash Avenue. It lasted less than a month, but twelve thousand people lined up to get in, readily paying a small entrance fee to see approximately three hundred works drawn from local collections of both American and European art. During the Civil War, Chicago philanthropists pioneered the idea of holding art exhibitions at sanitary fairs, although they received little credit for the idea after New York decided to do the same.

5 For more information on the Interstate Industrial Exposition's Art Gallery, see Kirsten M. Jensen, "'The American Salon': The Art Gallery at the Chicago Interstate Industrial Exposition, 1873–1890" (PhD diss., Graduate Center, City University of New York, 2007).

6 See Kirsten M. Jensen, "Her Sex Was an Insuperable Objection: Sara Hallowell and the Art Institute of Chicago" (MA thesis, Southern Connecticut State University, 2000).

7 "Art and Artists: The Exposition Pictures," *Chicago Inter-Ocean*, Sept. 13, 1883, 13.

8 "Monthly Record of American Art," *Magazine of Art* 8 (1885): 88.

9 Clarence A. Hough, "The Art Institute of Chicago," *Art & Archaeology* 12 (Sept.-Oct. 1921): 153.

10 William M. R. French to Sara Hallowell, Sept. 5, 1907, records of the director, The Art Institute of Chicago. In his letter, French expressed his hope that Hallowell, with her connections in Europe, particularly Paris, might be able to assist him in selecting works suitable for exhibition.

11 See William M. R. French to Frederic C. Bartlett, Sept. 13, 1907, records of the director, The Art Institute of Chicago. French wrote to Bartlett, a collector and artist who was also on the Art Institute's board, for advice in the matter: "Mr. Hutchinson and Mr. Ryerson thought 'Salome' pretty disagreeable and hesitated to give it a place. I write to ask you if you have a clear idea of the picture, and if so, whether as a member of the Art Committee, are in favor of exhibiting it."

12 William M. R. French to Emile Nolde, Dec. 30, 1907, records of the director, The Art Institute of Chicago. Nolde would later be included in the 1913 exhibition *Contemporary German Graphic Art*.

13 For French's comments, see William M. R. French to Halsey C. Ives, Sept. 17, 1908, records of the director, The Art Institute of Chicago.

14 "Chicago Leads All the World in Art!," Chicago *Examiner*, Oct. 3, 1908.

15 Ann Lee Morgan, "'A Modest Young Man with Theories': Arthur Dove in Chicago," in *The Old Guard and the Avant-Garde: Modernism in Chicago, 1910–1940*, ed. Sue Ann Prince (Chicago: University of Chicago Press, 1990), 23. Morgan discussed the difficulties involved in reconstructing with certainty the entire group of works shown due to the stylistic similarities of many of Dove's works, as well as the fact that many cannot be located. However, there are several that have been identified on the basis of contemporary descriptions. See ibid., 26–27.

16 H. Effa Webster, "Artist Dove Paints Rhythms of Color," *Chicago Examiner*, Mar. 15, 1912; and George Cram Cook, "Causerie; Post-Impressionism: After Seeing Mr. Dove's Pictures at Thurber's," *Chicago Evening Post Friday Literary Review*, Mar. 29, 1912, 1–2. See also Morgan (note 15), 30–32.

17 Morgan (note 15), 33.

18 Cook (note 16).

19 William M. R. French to Sara Hallowell, Feb. 3, 1912, records of the director, The Art Institute of Chicago. French's letter to Hallowell was written months before he entered into negotiations with the Association of American Painters and Sculptors for the Armory Show, in Dec. 1912.

20 John Rewald, *Cézanne and America: Dealers, Collectors, Artists and Critics* (Princeton, NJ: Princeton University Press, 1989), 11. Rewald noted that no Cézanne paintings had appeared in the ground-breaking Durand-Ruel exhibition in 1886 or in any of the subsequent Impressionist exhibits in New York, so Hallowell's introduction of two of Cézanne's paintings was indeed the first display of the artist's work in the United States. The two paintings were *Still Life with Milk Can, Carafe, and Coffee Bowl* (v. 337) (1879–80) and *Milk Can and Apples* (v. 338) (1879–90). The numbers refer to the entries in Lionello Venturi, *Cézanne: Son art, son oeuvre* (Paris: Paul Rosenberg, 1936).

21 See Maude Oliver, "Up-to-Date Tendency Shown in German Graphic Art and Henderson Exhibition," *Chicago Herald*, Jan. 12, 1913; Harriet Monroe, "Graphic Art Exhibit Shows German Versatility with Pen," *Chicago Tribune*, Jan. 12, 1913; and George B. Zug, untitled and undated clipping, scrapbooks, vols. 29–30 (reel 5), The Art Institute of Chicago.

22 Amy Paulding, "'Futurists' Startle by Hideous Lines," *Chicago Inter-Ocean*, Feb. 27, 1913. It should be noted that Paulding was not an art critic. Sue Ann Prince provided an excellent summation of the critical climate in Chicago during the Armory Show period in *The Old Guard and the Avant-Garde: Modernism in Chicago, 1910–1940*, ed. Sue Ann Prince (Chicago: University of Chicago Press, 1990), so I will not undertake to duplicate her work here.

23 George B. Zug, untitled and undated clipping, scrapbooks, vols. 29–30 (reel 5), The Art Institute of Chicago.
24 See "Cast out Picture; Stir Norwegians," *Chicago Daily Tribune*, Mar. 11, 1913. The painting was Bernhard Folkestad's *Summer Day*, a supposed barnyard scene that was apparently so shocking that women were reportedly averting their eyes and running away in horror. The painting may in fact have been Folkestad's *Sømmernatt* (1908; Statens Museum for Kunst, Copenhagen), which instead of a barnyard scene depicts a boy urinating from the door of a wooden structure.
25 Andrew Martinez, "A Mixed Reception for Modernism: The 1913 Armory Show at the Art Institute of Chicago," *Museum Studies* 19, no. 1 (1993): 34.
26 George B. Zug, untitled clipping, *Chicago Inter-Ocean*, Mar. 2, 1913, scrapbooks, vols. 29–30 (reel 5), The Art Institute of Chicago.
27 See William M. R. French to Charles L. Hutchinson, Mar. 5, 1913, and French to Dr. A. H. Fairbanks, Mar. 17, 1913, French correspondence, reel 27, The Art Institute of Chicago. Fairbanks was at the time director of the Boston Museum of Fine Arts, the next site on the exhibition's tour.
28 Ibid.
29 Sue Ann Prince, "'Of the Which and the Why of Daub and Smear': Chicago Critics Take on Modernism," in *The Old Guard and the Avant-Garde: Modernism in Chicago, 1910–1940*, ed. Sue Ann Prince (Chicago: University of Chicago Press, 1990), 97.
30 One exception is Sue Ann Prince, who noted that in general, "looking beyond the sensationalism of the headlines and the unparalleled moral outrage of non-arts writers, however, we find Chicago's response [to the Armory Show] to be more thoughtful, complex, and sophisticated than is generally acknowledged." Ibid., 98.
31 Sue Ann Prince noted that Monroe's articles in the conservative *Chicago Tribune* "reveal that she was far more astute than has been acknowledged by historians; they were consistently more measured, analytical, and positive than that of nearly any other American newspaper writer, whether in Chicago or New York." Ibid., 102.
32 Subcommittee of the Association of American Painters and Sculptors in Chicago, "The First Week of the International Exhibition of Modern Art in Chicago," Apr. 1, 1913, Elmer MacRae/Armory Show Papers, Hirshhorn Museum and Sculpture Garden, Smithsonian Institution.
33 Walter Kuhn to Elmer MacRae, Apr. 14, 1913, Elmer MacRae/Armory Show Papers, Hirshhorn Museum and Sculpture Garden, Smithsonian Institution.

LATENT IMAGES
CLAIMING CHICAGO'S EXTRAORDINARY PHOTOGRAPHIC LEGACY

Lynne Warren

This is not so much an essay about Chicago photography or photography in Chicago as it is an essay about Chicago as a great, yet often perplexing city. Chicago is a funny place. It has defined itself in so many different areas—through poetry, machine politics, the Prohibition gangster, the skyscraper, gospel music and urban blues, rough-scrabble journalism, and mail-order mercantilism. In recent decades, Chicago-generated genres and fields of thought have become world standards, including the Chicago school of economics, improv theater, house music, and molecular gastronomy. Yet at the same time, and in some very important ways, Chicago has been defined by others, most significantly for the fine arts through its designation as the "Second City." In 1952 A. J. Liebling published a series of three articles in *The New Yorker* in which he characterized Chicago as a provincial backwater. To Liebling, and by extension many New Yorkers, Chicago had little or no sophistication, both in its urban quality—even its world-famous architecture was portrayed as a Hollywood facade that ran along the lakefront and hid the dreary "real Chicago"—and in its cultural and intellectual offerings.[1] Although adapted by Chicagoans trying to make the best of it—most appropriately by its nose-thumbing, world-renowned comedy troupe—the name Second City was never meant to be laudatory and unfortunately crystallized a set of assumptions that for decades has cast a long shadow.

As this project demonstrates, Chicago is still unfortunately insecure, particularly in the visual arts, and laboring under a "second-city" complex. An especially interesting example of this wrongful insecurity appears in Chicago photography. Around the world, Chicago's contribution to twentieth-century photography is recognized as seminal, in large part due to Hungarian-born László Moholy-Nagy and the heritage that resulted from the direct and indirect influence of the Institute of Design (ID), which he founded in 1937 as the New Bauhaus. Moholy was well known and respected as an experimental artist in Europe when he was hired by a group of progressive Chicago industrialists and merchants whose desire was not to create a fine-arts school but to found a laboratory for training industrial designers. Ironically, this school—geared toward developing "the whole individual" to contribute creatively to society through the intersection of art, design, science, and technology—became the foundation for an extraordinary fine-arts flowering in Chicago.[2] Because of ID, Chicago was home to two of the towering photographers of the post–World War II era, Harry Callahan and Aaron Siskind. And because of Callahan's and Siskind's presence at ID, Chicago has produced literally dozens of world-renowned figures in the field of photography, both fine artists and important teachers who spread the school's methods and philosophy around the country and the world. These include Barbara Crane (see **FIG. 3.1**), Yasuhiro Ishimoto, Kenneth Josephson, Ray K. Metzker, Richard Nickel, Art Sinsabaugh, and others who came to Chicago because of its reputation as a fine-arts photography center.[3] Yet ask a Chicagoan to name the city's most famous historical artist and the chance that you will hear in reply the names of László

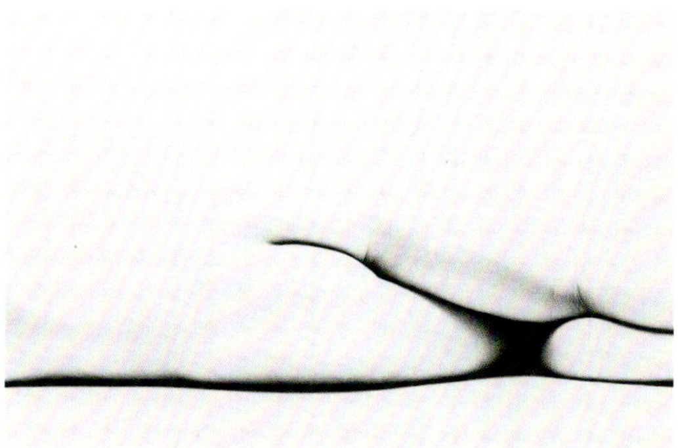

3.1 Barbara Crane (American, born 1928). *Human Form*, 1966. Gelatin silver print; 5 ½ × 8 ½ in. Stephen Daiter Gallery, Chicago.

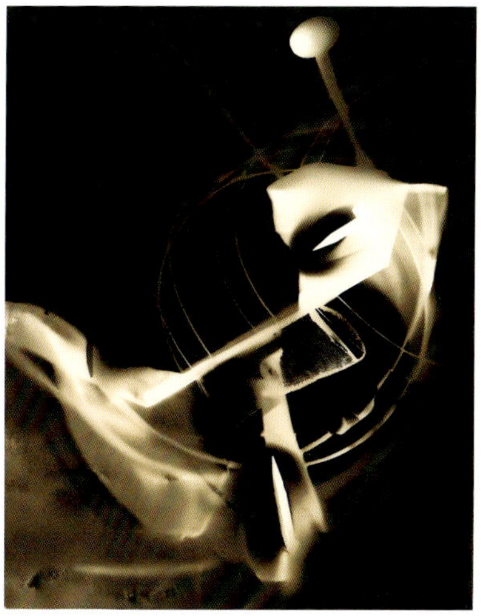

3.2 László Moholy-Nagy (American, born Hungary, 1895–1946). *Untitled*, c. 1940. Gelatin silver photogram; 19 ½ × 15 ¾ in. The Art Institute of Chicago, gift of George and Ruth Barford, 1968.264.

Moholy-Nagy, Harry Callahan, Aaron Siskind, or any other Chicago photographer is a remote one.

Moholy, along with his German Bauhaus colleagues, believed art had important utilitarian, pedagogical, and moral functions and should be used toward a holistic betterment of society. These notions were in direct opposition to the nineteenth-century belief in "art for art's sake" that surrounded much modern art, and they in fact structure the current international contemporary-art dialogue. Moholy's establishment of the Light Workshop as an integral part of his New Bauhaus curriculum set in motion the extraordinary chain of events and relationships that is the Chicago photographic tradition, with its emphasis on experimentation and the documentation of urban spaces and people. His work with his famous "Light-Space Modulator" machines to create abstract photograms (see **FIG. 3.2**) represents perhaps the quintessential ID style. Moholy also brought a German Bauhaus colleague, György Kepes, to head the Light Workshop from 1937 to 1943; Kepes made some of his most striking photographic works in Chicago, including solarized exposures of his wife, Juliet. He went on to become a seminal figure in American art and technology, founding the Center for Advanced Visual Studies at the Massachusetts Institute of Technology.

The strange neglect of Chicago's great photographic traditions by the larger art community can also be said to have begun, in a sense, with Moholy. His contributions as a theorist, educator, and thinker through his seminal text *Vision in Motion* may have overshadowed his artistic contributions in general, though in Chicago his radical experimentation was celebrated by the legendary exhibition *Art by Telephone* (1969), held at the Museum of Contemporary Art. This exhibition referred to a 1927 piece in which Moholy telephoned instructions for a painting to a colleague who created the work. Other shows have focused on the artist's paintings or photographic innovations. However, during his Chicago years, Moholy also experimented extensively with a Leica camera, including very early use of color slide film (Kodachrome). This revolutionary color work has languished, remaining largely unexhibited in his estate until a recent unveiling at a New York gallery.[4]

Callahan is another perplexing example of the Chicago art community's blank spot when it comes to photography. Universally recognized as one of the premier artists of the twentieth century, he remains little heralded in his hometown, where he taught and made much of his best-known work, including mesmerizing photographs of his wife, Eleanor. Callahan also made highly experimental multiple-exposure pictures, collage studies using images scavenged from magazines, and other advanced work. A small but telling demonstration of our town's amnesia when it comes to Callahan: in March 2011, Pace/MacGill Gallery in New York mounted a comparison of the work of Callahan and Jackson Pollock, as both moved toward abstraction in the late 1940s and 1950s. Most members of Chicago's art world were oblivious to this widely praised exhibition, in contrast to the much heralded, well-attended exhibition of Ed Paschke's work mounted in 2010 at Gagosian Gallery, also in New York. And while Callahan, who worked and

3.3 Aaron Siskind (American, 1903–1991). *Chicago 22*, 1957. Gelatin silver print; 10 ½ × 13 ⅓ in. The Art Institute of Chicago, gift of Emanuel and Edithann M. Gerard, 1991.1016.

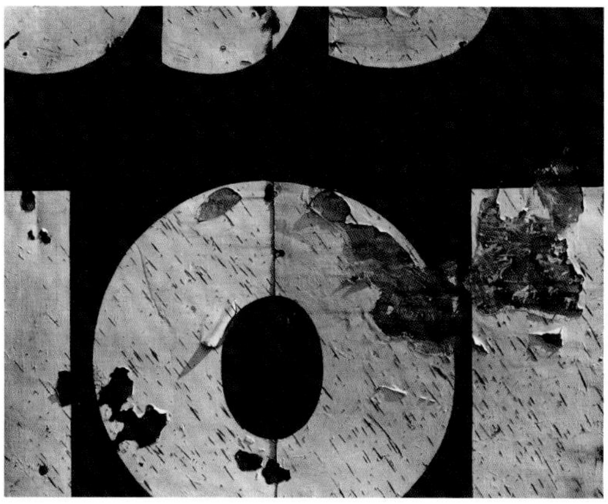

lived in Chicago in the 1940s and 1950s, may seem long ago and far away, Chicago's art community continues to claim painter Leon Golub, who was born and bred in Chicago but spent little time here beyond his schooling in the late 1940s, and sculptor H. C. Westermann, who studied and lived in Chicago for barely a decade before decamping to Connecticut in 1961.

Siskind is another major figure who spent much of his career living and teaching in Chicago. His position as a pioneer of abstraction in the 1940s—realized through extreme close-ups of urban signage (see **FIG. 3.3**), graffiti, peeling paint, and other "found" opportunities—won him immediate recognition and recommended him to Callahan, who hired him to teach at ID in 1951. Siskind, considered an important link to the larger art world, especially Abstract Expressionist painting, was extremely prolific during his Chicago years and maintained a close friendship with Callahan. He and Callahan are often thought of as opposites—Callahan working representationally and Siskind abstractly—yet both men completed significant bodies of work that explored both ends of this spectrum. Siskind made his influential *Pleasures and Terrors of Levitation* series, showing a man's body in midair, in the 1950s. He also participated in architectural projects, including photographing Adler and Sullivan buildings and Mies van der Rohe interiors, in collaboration with students.

Nathan Lerner and Arthur Siegel, important early students in the Light Workshop, also eventually became influential photography instructors at ID. Lerner was an extraordinary abstract and Surrealist photographer. His pioneering social documentation of Maxwell Street in the late 1930s identifies him as one of the founders of the genre of Chicago street photography later explored so brilliantly by his ID colleague Callahan.[5] Numerous other practitioners—from Art Shay, who poignantly chronicled the Chicago of Nelson Algren (cat. 37) and his lover, Simone de Beauvoir; to recently discovered self-taught photographer Vivian Maier—have also worked in this genre. Another influential member of Chicago's photographic community, Siegel created one of the iconic images of the twentieth century—the extraordinary crowd shot *Right of Assembly*—and was also an early practitioner of color street photography. It was he who brought Callahan, a fellow native of Detroit, to Chicago.

• • •

It is not that the history of photography in Chicago has gone unexplored. Numerous exhibitions and books—including *The New Vision: Forty Years of Photography at the Institute of Design*, *Taken by Design: Photography from the Institute of Design, 1937–1971*, and *Harry Callahan: The Photographer at Work*—explore both the overall history and the individual artists of the Chicago photographic tradition. *Chicago Photographs*, drawn from the significant photography collection of the LaSalle Bank (now the Bank of America collection), brought together the pictures of local, national, and international figures who have worked in Chicago. The Chicago-based photography gallery Stephen Daiter has long championed the Chicago school of

3.4 Kenneth Josephson (American, born 1932). *Chicago, 1972*, 1972. Gelatin silver print and postcard collage; 4 3/4 × 7 in. Museum of Contemporary Art, Chicago, gift of the Foster Charitable Trust in memory of Reuben A. Foster, 1983.37.

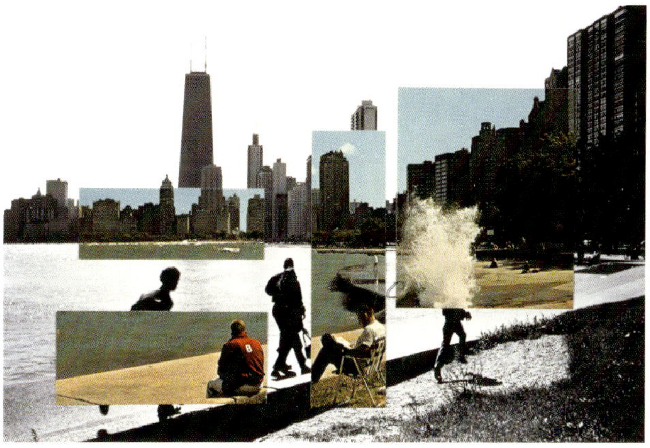

photography, and Edward Houk Gallery, which opened in Chicago in 1980 and in 1991 relocated to New York, displayed the work of major international photographers, providing a fitting context for Moholy-Nagy, whom the gallery represented. From the 1970s into the 1990s, Carol Ehlers brought her discerning eye to the Chicago arts scene, first at the Allan Frumkin Gallery in the late 1970s and then in her own spaces, from which she championed Callahan and others.[6] The Art Institute of Chicago has a huge and important photography collection and has frequently mounted exhibitions of Chicago interest, including the 2002 *Taken by Design*.

Yet in recent years, it seems non-Chicago galleries and museums more frequently focus on the seminal contributions of Chicago's photographers than the local institutions whose mission it is to reach and educate the wider art community.[7] The problem may be that members of Chicago's art community are unaccustomed to thinking about historical photography—photography before it was transformed into just another art medium by Cindy Sherman, Andreas Gursky, and others—when the notion of important Chicago artists arises. This is not necessarily a syndrome unique to Chicago. Photographers have long been limited by the fact of their medium as a specialty with its own audiences, museum departments, and collectors. For example, as experimental as he was, Callahan was a photographer through and through. With his multiple exposures of architectural elements, he pioneered the exploration of the technical capabilities of the camera and film to create abstract images. Yet these are still seen as photographs, made in the context of photography rather than larger art-historical movements. Only in recent years have contemporary artists such as Walead Beshty, using photographic means, followed up on such innovations and brought abstract photography to a larger audience. Indeed, Callahan's figurative work, whether street shots such as DePaul Art Museum's *Untitled* (cat. 10) or portraits of his wife, is foundational to contemporary artist-photographers as disparate in style as Peter Hujar and Philip-Lorca diCorcia, both of whose work has a strong following in the international art world.

Two other Chicago artists whose adherence to the classical world of photography has restricted their recognition in the wider art world are Josephson (see **FIG. 3.4**) and Robert Heinecken. Josephson is one of the founders of conceptual photography and has spent his career in Chicago since arriving to attend ID in 1958. His *Images within Images* series, which he began in the 1960s, prefigured an entire genre of contemporary art making that explores the deceptions that photographs can achieve with stunning reality. Although primarily associated with Los Angeles, Heinecken spent almost half his time in Chicago from the 1980s until 1996, teaching at the School of the Art Institute of Chicago; upon retirement he relocated to the city full-time. He was a pioneering image scavenger, using readymade photographs taken from magazines, advertising, and other commercial sources, though he has been overshadowed by his colleague John Baldessari.

Many in the Chicago art community may not realize that the city was also literally a nexus

3.5 Walker Evans (American, 1903–1975). *Chicago*, 1946. Gelatin silver print; 2 ¼ × 2 ¼ in. Collection of the DePaul Art Museum, 2011.4.

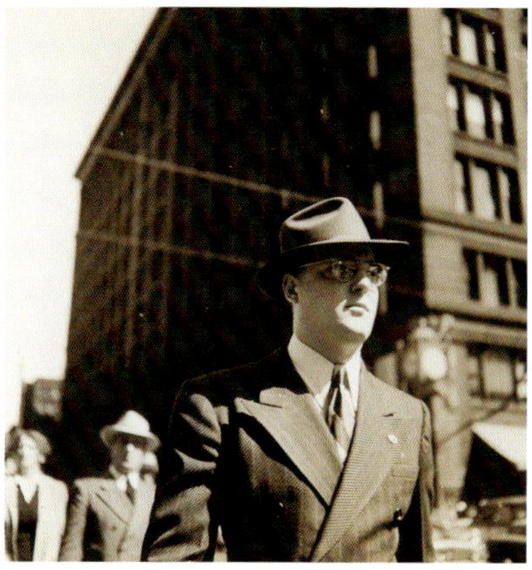

3.6 Henri Cartier-Bresson (French, 1908–2004). *Chicago*, 1947. Magnum Photos.

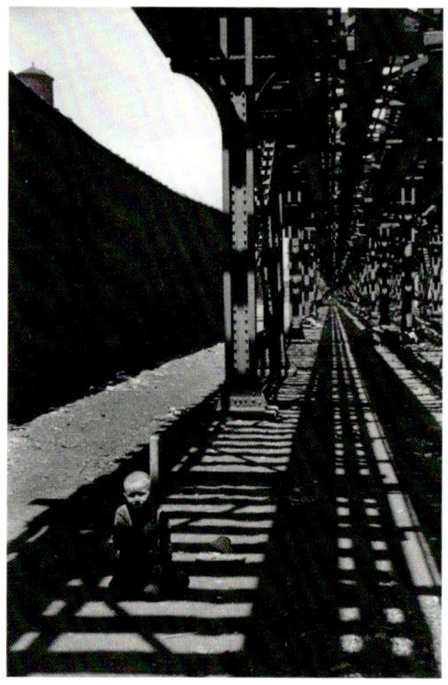

for important non-Chicago photographers in the twentieth century. As a prototypical American city with a central location in the United States, it was a natural destination for national and international photographers for whom travel was an essential component of their practice. Walker Evans astutely photographed the city on assignment from *Fortune* magazine in the 1940s (see **FIG 3.5**). In 1947, on a cross-continental tour, Henri Cartier-Bresson included a stop in Chicago, where he created classic photographs of life in the city, including a view of a child beneath heavily shadowed El tracks (**FIG. 3.6**), which was reproduced in his seminal 1952 book *The Decisive Moment*. In the 1950s, Robert Frank made some of his most iconic images in Chicago for his book *The Americans*, including *Political Rally, Chicago*, which depicts a tuba player beneath American-flag bunting.

Other long-term visitors to the city include Ishimoto, an American-born Japanese photographer who studied at ID with Callahan and Siskind. Considered an important link between American and Japanese photography, his photographic portrait of the city, *Chicago, Chicago*, created when he lived in Chicago between 1958 and 1961, presents compelling images of everyday citizens and hardscrabble cityscapes in a document of great social and historic value (**FIG. 3.7**). In the 1960s, Danny Lyon made important work in Chicago in his unsparing documentary style. Garry Winogrand, who was a guest teacher at ID in the 1970s, pioneered his style of casual, seemingly haphazard portraits within the urban landscape of Chicago.

More recently, a roster of top contemporary artists who use photography has completed important work in Chicago. Initially traveling to Chicago for an exhibition at the Renaissance Society, the German photographer Thomas Struth shot the city in 1990, including color studies of the trading pits of the Chicago Board of Trade, which his countryman Andreas Gursky also famously photographed in 1999. Japanese photographer Toshio Shibata and Los Angeles–based Catherine Opie were both commissioned by the Museum of Contemporary Art to create new works. In 2001, under the patronage of the Art Institute, German artist Vera Lutter completed important images in her large-scale camera-obscura series in Chicago.

Chicago is also the birthplace of architectural photography, led by Hedrich-Blessing Architectural Photographers. Founded in 1929 to provide services to Chicago's great architectural firms, Hedrich-Blessing brought the utilitarian practice of documenting buildings to a new, fine-arts level, not only in Chicago but also around the world. Chicago's status as a city of great architecture has attracted such practitioners as Nickel, who famously died while scavenging architectural fragments during the razing of Louis Sullivan's Chicago Stock Exchange, and, more recently, the eminent Japanese artist Hiroshi Sugimoto, who made haunting portrayals of Marina Towers and the Museum of Contemporary Art.

And finally, in the arena of photographic education and advancement, the modern concept of the photographic seminar was begun at ID in 1946, when administrators and historians joined

3.7 Yasuhiro Ishimoto (Japanese, born United States, 1921). *#17, Chicago*, 1959/61. Gelatin silver print; 14 × 11 in. The Art Institute of Chicago, gift of Yasuhiro and Shigeru Ishimoto, 1999.90.

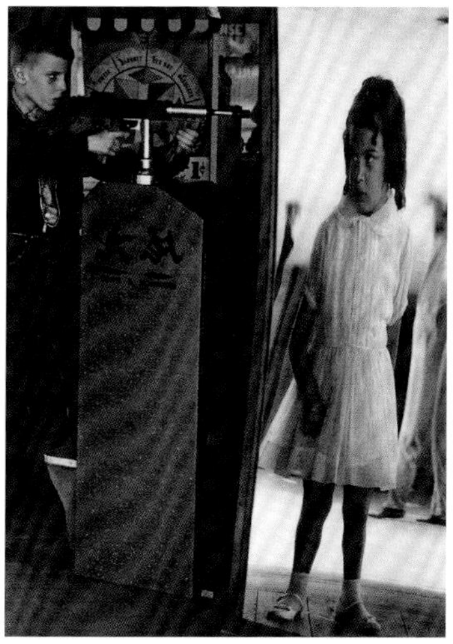

photographers representing a broad spectrum of specialties for a summer workshop. The pioneering New York–based photographer Berenice Abbott; the Dada experimenter Erwin Blumenfeld; the formalist Paul Strand; *Life* magazine staff photographer Frank Scherschel (who had recently returned from covering World War II in Europe); noted crime photographer Weegee; the overseer of the photo documentary project for the Farm Security Administration (FSA), Roy Styker; and curator and historian Beaumont Newhall comprised the eminent group, which was completed by ID staff, including Callahan and Siegel, the workshop's organizer.[8] The significance of such disparate figures coming together, especially in a time of limited communication among artists from different areas of the country, cannot be overstated for its impact on the exchange of ideas and subsequent developments in the field. A similar gathering of colleagues—including those with ID ties, such as Josephson, Sinsabaugh, Siskind, and Henry Holmes Smith—in Rochester, New York, in 1962 was the genesis of the Society for Photographic Education, a leading organization for photography in the United States, which held its inaugural meeting in Chicago in 1963.

It is long past time for Chicago to enthusiastically and proudly embrace our great photographic traditions and artists. With strong programs at the School of the Art Institute and Columbia College (although no longer at ID, which effectively discontinued its photography program in the 1980s), young talent is continually emerging in or relocating to Chicago.[9] If photography was and is of major significance in the history of art in the United States, and indeed the world, and is an important contemporary-art medium, Chicago's contributions to the field must be well known and appreciated in the city. Perhaps the younger generations of artist-photographers, in blurring the lines between photography and other contemporary-art media, will actually clarify Chicago's visual-arts heritage.

ENDNOTES

1 Liebling started the first of the articles ("So Proud To Be Jammy-Jammy") by describing what must be Oak Street Beach. He looked up at the city from the vantage point of an imaginary "beacher" (a female who is "comparing the discolorations of [her] legs with those of other girls"). He went on to say, "But the beachers are not fooled. They know that what they see is like a theatre backdrop with a city painted on it." In Liebling's foreword to the book compiling the three articles, which was published in 1952, he described letters of complaint he received from Chicagoans, including one who asked, "Is Mr. Liebling forming a 'Be Nasty to Chicago Club'???" Admittedly, Liebling was a humorist and much of his analysis was satirical, but few in the Windy City took it that way. See Liebling, *Chicago: The Second City* (Lincoln: University of Nebraska Press, 2004), 7.

2 For a more detailed history of ID, see Peter Selz, "Modernism Comes to Chicago: The Institute of Design," in Lynne Warren, *Art in Chicago, 1945–1995* (Chicago/New York: Museum of Contemporary Art/Thames and Hudson, 1996). Exhibition catalog; and David Travis et al., *Taken by Design: Photographs from The Institute of Design, 1937–1971* (Chicago: Art Institute of Chicago/University of Chicago Press, 2001). Exhibition catalog.

3 Other important photographic teachers and practitioners who were educated in Chicago or have been longtime Chicago residents include Harold Allen

(head of the Photography Department at the School of the Art Institute of Chicago [SAIC]), Tom Arndt, David Avison, Thomas Barrow (professor at the University of New Mexico), Dawoud Bey (professor at Columbia College), Patty Carroll (professor at ID and SAIC), Alan Cohen (professor at ID and SAIC), Linda Conner (professor at the San Francisco Art Institute), Barbara DeGenevieve (professor at SAIC), François Deschamps, Terry Evans, Scott Fortino, William Frederking (professor at Columbia College), John Grimes (long associated with ID), Doug Ischar (professor at University of Illinois at Chicago and SAIC), Joseph Jachna (professor at ID and University of Illinois Chicago Circle), Barbara Kasten (professor at Columbia College), Lewis Kostiner, Peter LeGrand (professor at Columbia College), William Larson, Herbert Migdoll, Wayne Miller, Joyce Neimanas (department head and professor at SAIC), Esther Parada (long associated with University of Illinois at Chicago), Robert A. Sengstacke, Victor Skrebneski, Keith A. Smith, Joseph Sterling (professor at ID and SAIC; established the photography program at Columbia College), Robert Stiegler (long associated with University of Illinois at Chicago), Charles Swedlund (professor at Southern Illinois University-Carbondale), Brad Temkin, Bob Thall (former department head at Columbia College), Charles Traub (long associated with the School of Visual Arts, New York), and Jay Wolke. Allen, Avison, Barrow, Carroll, Cohen, Conner, Grimes, Jachna, Kostiner, LeGrand, Larson, Miller, Parada, Smith, Sterling, Stiegler, Swedlund, and Traub were trained at ID. This list is by no means a definitive one.

4 A number of Moholy's color photographs were featured in two exhibitions in the Andrea Rosen Gallery in 2002 and 2007. Three of these astonishing color works were shown in the Art Institute of Chicago's 2002 *Taken by Design* exhibition, including abstract images of lights at night.

5 Lerner's creative output unfortunately has been overshadowed by his role as the discoverer and benefactor of Henry Darger.

6 Ehlers also curated the extraordinary 2010 exhibition *Moholy: An Education of the Senses* at the Loyola University Museum of Art.

7 A major Callahan retrospective, *Variations*, was held at the Fondation Henri-Cartier Bresson in Paris in July–Nov. 2010.

8 Charles Traub, *The New Vision: Forty Years of Photography at the Institute of Design* (Millerton, NY: Aperture Books, 1982), 75.

9 Those who can be considered twenty-first-century figures include Scott Dietrich, Ken Fandell, Rashid Johnson, Jason Lazarus, New Catalogue, Melanie Schiff, Anna Shteynshleyger, and Brian Ulrich, to name but a few.

ABJECT POP IN CHICAGO

Robert Cozzolino

Before the rise of Andy Warhol, the most famous example of an American artist immersed in popular culture was the Chicagoan Ivan Albright. Impressed by Albright's work, director Albert Lewin commissioned him to paint a portrait of Dorian Gray for his 1945 film adaptation of Oscar Wilde's *The Picture of Dorian Gray*. Upon seeing his beauty depicted in a portrait, Gray declares that he will give his soul to remain youthful while the picture ages in his place. This wish comes true, but the picture records more than Gray's aging—it also reveals his moral decay. Albright's climactic image of the spiritually debased Gray provided an effective cinematic shock and became the best-known painting of his career (**FIG. 4.1**). Already famous before the commission, Albright was a favorite with national journalists, who dubbed him the "court jester of American art" because his wit and public-relations savvy contrasted with the macabre content of his work. From 1941 to 1946, he often appeared in mass-circulation magazines such as *Life*, *Newsweek, Time*, and *Vogue,* all of which ran articles in connection with *The Picture of Dorian Gray*, his other work, and his personal life.[1]

Ivan's twin brother, Malvin, accompanied him to Hollywood to paint the portrait of the unblemished Gray. Playing up the novelty of twins painting beautiful and debauched versions of the same character, hundreds of newspapers ran features on the artists, while nationally syndicated gossip columns covered their Hollywood antics. They responded by willfully exploiting the popular image of the artist as comic/eccentric throughout their Hollywood residency. Indeed, coverage of the Albright twins kept Lewin's film in the national press on a monthly basis for a year and a half prior to its release.[2] Despite the popular acclaim this episode brought to Albright—and to Chicago's art world—he grew disgusted by his Hollywood work and tried to disown it for the rest of his life. In his view, the portrait of Gray was "commercial" and made under artificial time constraints.[3]

There was tension in Albright's repulsion over having *become* popular culture. In reality he negotiated an astonishing amount of freedom in his commissions and exploited national attention for his own self-promotion. Art collector and advertising executive Earle Ludgin took notice of this latter skill when he remarked to Albright that he was "not only the fine artist we always said you were—but the finest publicity man the art world has ever seen. . . . I open all the magazines now, expecting you to pop out of *Boys' Life*, *Country Gentleman* or *True Comics*."[4]

Albright's engagement with popular culture and subsequent characterization of that experience as abject set a tone for how artists in Chicago used and negotiated popular culture in later generations.[5] Albright selectively employed bloody, Gothic tropes of cinematic horror, worked from a subjective vision in designing his pictures, and tackled themes that were extensions of his independent work, engaging popular culture and using it for his own ends. Yet he was careful to draw attention away from anything that might appear appropriated from popular culture and to emphasize the independent, less-conventional aspects of his work.

For much of its history, Chicago's art world has valued individuality and rejected trends.[6]

4.1 Ivan Albright (American, 1897–1983). *The Picture of Dorian Gray*, 1943–44. Oil on canvas; 85 3/4 × 42 1/4 in. The Art Institute of Chicago, gift of Ivan Albright, 1977.21.

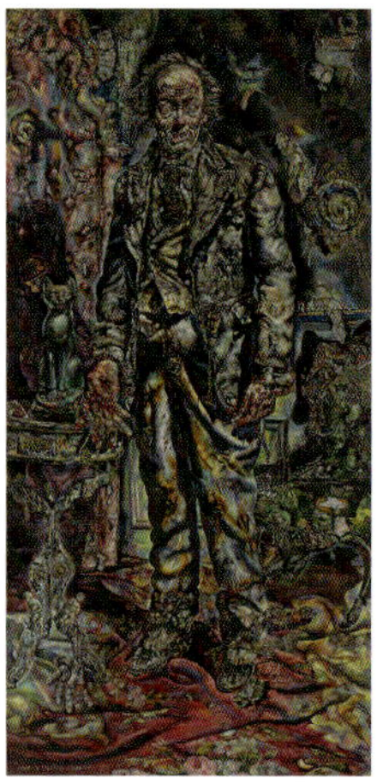

4.2 Karl Wirsum (American, born 1939). Page from *The Hairy Who Sideshow*, 1967, published for the second Hairy Who group exhibition at the Hyde Park Art Center, Chicago, February 24–March 24, 1967. Courtesy of the Roger Brown Study Collection, School of the Art Institute of Chicago.

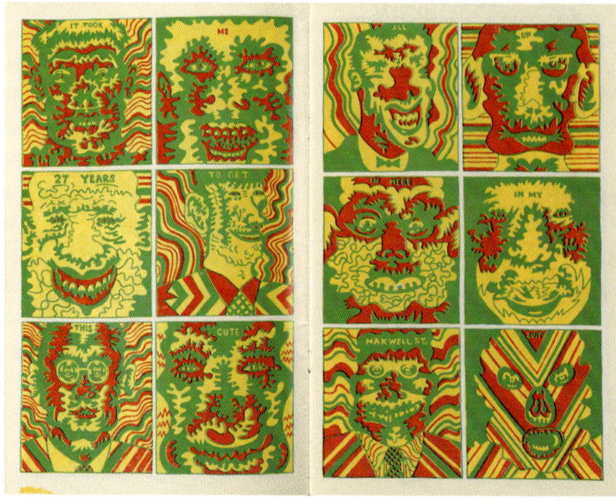

An intensely personal and challenging quality to art in Chicago has often led critics and art historians to avoid integrating the city's artists into histories of Pop Art, even when their context would be made richer and their arguments strengthened by including the achievements of these artists. Claes Oldenburg steered an important early conversation on his interest in Pop subjects toward Chicago in order to correct his interviewer's assumptions about the primacy of New York in this movement. He said:

> There is always a lot of communication between artists because the art world is a very small one and you can sense what other people are doing. Besides, America has a traditional interest in pop culture. In Chicago, where I spent a lot of time, people like June Leaf and George Cohen were working very close to a Pop medium in 1952. George Cohen used to go to the dime store and buy all the dolls he could find and other stuff like that. Even though he used them for his own personal image there has always been this tendency.[7]

Oldenburg's version of Pop developed from his early life in Chicago as a reporter for the City News Bureau, when he experienced the city's strong collections of Surrealism and its embrace of Jean Dubuffet's art. Consider him a representative artist of the Chicago diaspora to New York. His Pop was messy, absurd, perversely funny, and at turns tragic. Its existentialist tenor is reflected in his 1961 "Statement," a tour de force of evocative, declarative writing in which he laid out his belief in the capacity for real life to bring art into existence: accidents, bodily fluids, evidence of mortality, "kids' smells" and sensations, "soggy onions," "the brown sad art of rotting apples," "bread wet by rain," "the sweat that develops between crossed legs," sensory experience, the visceral, and the lived. "I am for an art which is eaten, like a piece of pie, or abandoned with great contempt, like a piece of shit," he intoned, leaving no ambiguity about the centrality of the body to meaning in the world—gloriously abject, unmistakably real.[8]

Indeed, in further describing the distinctive way in which Chicago artists viewed and used popular culture, the artist Roger Brown said: "[Here] one sees [comics and advertising] as art in themselves, not as something to be blown up to make art, but as something to parallel in your own work. Those things are already art: so if you can make art as good, you're really lucky."[9] Karl Wirsum, for whom the multisensory spectacles of Riverside Amusement Park and the Maxwell Street Market were important, absorbed comics and advertising but reinterpreted them in his own voice (cat. 41). He grew up on Dick Tracy and wanted to be a comic-strip artist. A spread he contributed to the comic *The Hairy Who Sideshow* (**FIG. 4.2**) presents a kaleidoscopic procession of twelve neon-lit late-night characters whose faces transform into ritual masks. Early on, after studying changes in the styles of his beloved comic strips, he noted:

> The idea of developing your own approach was important. . . . I started to think about it and it's very much the idea of personalizing . . . taking an inspiration, something that you're

4.3 Paul Thek (American, 1933–1988). *Meat Piece with Warhol Brillo Box*, 1965, from the series *Technological Reliquaries*. Beeswax, painted wood, and Plexiglas; 14 × 17 × 17 in. Philadelphia Museum of Art; purchased with funds contributed by the Daniel W. Dietrich Foundation, 1990-111-1.

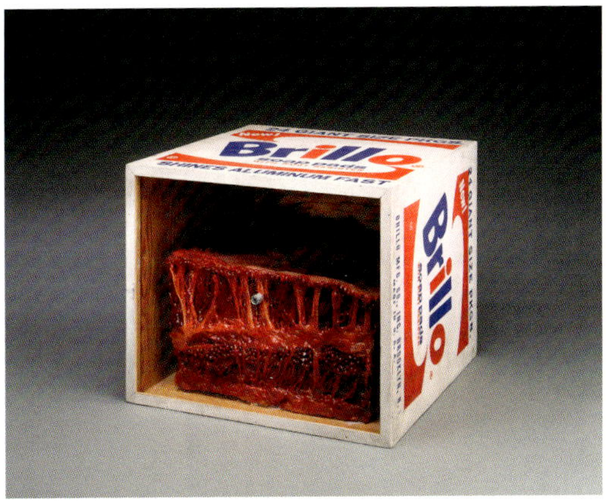

4.4 Peter Saul (American, born 1934). *Saigon*, 1967. Acrylic, enamel, and oil on canvas; 92 ¾ × 142 in. Whitney Museum of American Art, New York, Purchase, with funds from the Friends of the Whitney Museum of American Art, 69.103.

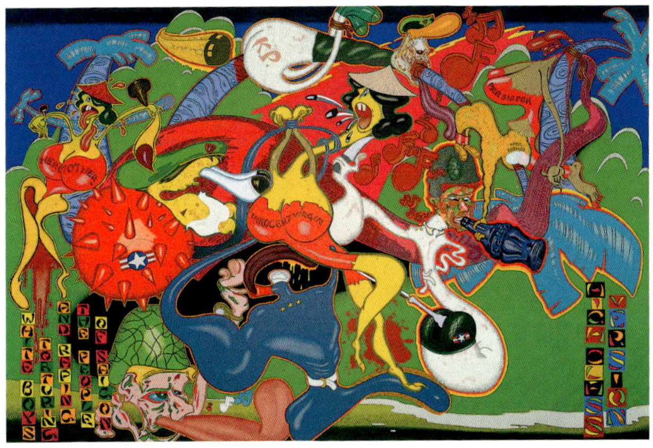

> enthused with and then bringing your own force to it. Just copying it wasn't appealing to me. So as a young kid, I didn't copy "Dick Tracy" but created my own criminals and things.[10]

In the late 1960s, Chicagoan Ray Yoshida perversely mined indexed specimens from comics, arranging endless, irregular rows of uniformed torsos discreetly missing limbs and heads, or with those appendages replaced by phantom hands and feet or outsized arms. More mysteriously, he placed crumpled and soiled funny pages into Lucite boxes, their disorder pinned beneath grids to form comic shrines. Yoshida's approach honors the comics he loved while playfully subverting their narrative clarity and graphic legibility.

These uses of popular culture for personal and often psychologically challenging purposes expose a willfully abject dimension to Pop Art that projects far from the "cool" it is alleged to embody. The luridly spectral image of Dorian Gray that Albright produced for the Hollywood film may be the earliest example of this quality. Artists working in Chicago played an important role in developing this critical and confrontational relationship between art and American mass culture, whether or not they considered themselves Pop artists. This may be why Peter Saul's early paintings of cartoon characters murderously brandishing axes, anthropomorphic toilets, intestines, excrement, floating penises, and gun-toting maniacs met with success in Chicago (despite the fact that Saul never worked there) but were gradually held in greater suspicion in New York, never fully admitted into the Pop club. By 1964 critic Ellen Johnson declared that Saul was "stripping things of their insipid packaging and putting them bluntly as they are," employing mass-media images to achieve a "natural radiant vulgarity" by using the language of advertising to undermine its claims to truth and altruism.[11]

By the mid-1960s, there were ample signs that American artists recognized the capacity for popular-culture subjects to dig deeper and that there were alarming things scurrying out from beneath the surface of everyday life. In 1965 New York–based artist Paul Thek acquired a wooden Brillo box sculpture from Andy Warhol and flipped it over on one of its long sides to reveal a dark void. Thek filled it with a wax and pigment sculpture that uncannily resembled a bloody slab of raw flesh freshly excised from an indeterminate creature and allowed to fester within a makeshift reliquary (**FIG. 4.3**). *Meat Piece with Warhol Brillo Box* retains the visceral power to horrify viewers with its abject presentation of glistening remains, and Thek's choice of container demands scrutiny. By 1965 Warhol had expanded his repertoire beyond commercial products, comics, and celebrities to include devastatingly unfiltered silkscreen paintings of electric chairs, food poisoning, police brutality, bodies mutilated in car crashes, and suicides. He had shifted his focus from American mass media to the bigger picture of mass experience and the places in which capitalist abundance and prosperity fell apart.

Thek's *Meat Piece* makes Warhol's engagement with the catastrophes of modern society explicit. It exposes the persistent dark and absurdly grotesque aspects of American media culture that

4.5 Dominick Di Meo (American, born 1927). *Landscape Beautification Johnson Style*, c. 1967. Photomechanical print on paper; 10 × 8 in. Courtesy of the artist.

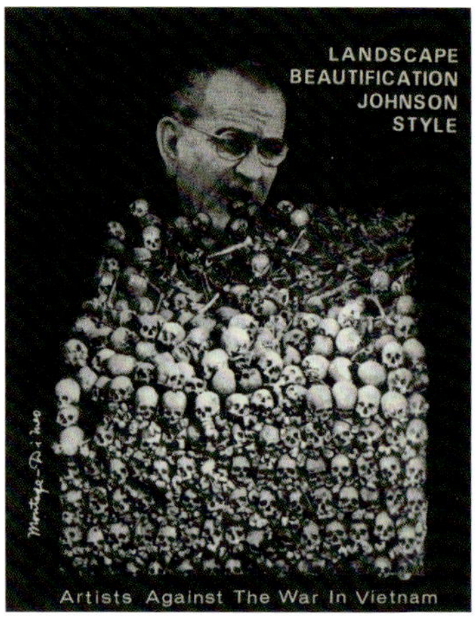

4.6 Ed Paschke (American, 1939–2004). *Tet Inoffensive*, 1968. Oil on canvas; 39 × 35 in. Collection of Robert Bergman.

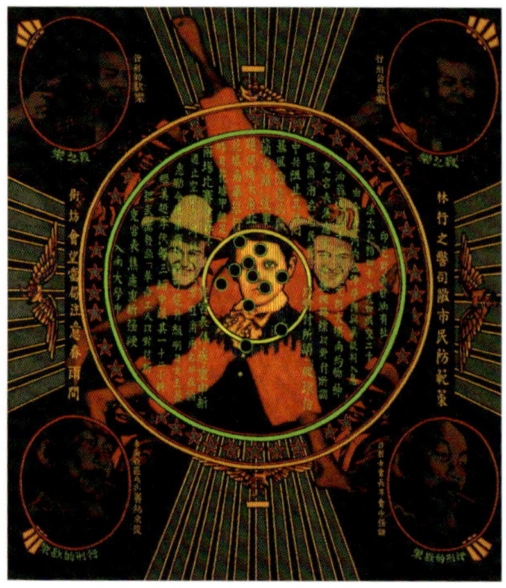

many artists examined in Chicago and beyond.[12] For example, Saul's *Vietnam* series of 1964–70 boldly accused the Johnson administration of atrocities and leveraging cinematic thrills from destruction (**FIG. 4.4**). Saul wrote to his dealer, Allan Frumkin:

> My soldier is a dirty freak; he avoids the enemy; his object is to get around the enemy, to sneak into his camp, rape his women, commit perversion on children, rob banks. . . .
> I wouldn't dignify war by any picturing of actual combat which would include men shooting bullets at each other. . . . This is dehumanization: people are what you use them for.[13]

In Chicago around the same time, Dominick Di Meo made a savagely effective antiwar photomontage (**FIG. 4.5**) criticizing what he and others felt had become President Johnson's campaign of death in Southeast Asia. Di Meo distributed the image as a leaflet to people on the street, getting his message directly into their hands. Playing on First Lady Ladybird Johnson's mass-media campaign to "beautify" America's highways, Di Meo juxtaposed her husband's familiar visage with a wedge of skulls from a catacomb. The media can cover superficial cleanup initiatives at home, Di Meo seemed to say, but it cannot purge the tragedy unfolding in Vietnam.

Ed Paschke's *Tet Inoffensive* (**FIG. 4.6**), which alludes to a devastating turning point against the United States in the Vietnam War, is a brutal indictment of the celebration and repetition of violence in the media that had become prominent in the 1960s. At the top left and right of the painting, the artist reproduced a famously horrific image that won its photographer, Eddie Adams, a Pulitzer Prize: General Nguyen Ngoc Loan shooting a Vietcong guerilla point blank. Mirroring that murder are two images of Ho Chi Minh, pictured confidently smoking with a smirk on his face. Paschke married this to a critique of American imperialism, made explicit in the center through cinematic images of cowboys.

Thus, from their earliest engagement with popular culture, Chicago artists embraced an aesthetic of the abject, which they used to frame (politically) or infect (through transformation) the pristine ads and kid-friendly comics that inspired them. The abject particularly characterizes the relationship that Chicago artists who emerged in the late 1960s had with popular-culture imagery. It is manifested through an intense focus on subjects that simultaneously fascinate and horrify, especially imagery that foregrounds the pathetic materiality of the human body, its limits, and its mortality. The frequent permeation into consciousness and daily life of these base bodily functions, excessive growths, rot, sexual deviancy, or psychological disorder parallels how philosopher Julia Kristeva theorized the abject. She wrote:

> These body fluids, this defilement, this shit are what life withstands, hardly and with difficulty, on the part of death. There I am at the border of my condition as a living being. My body extricates itself, as being alive, from that border. Such wastes drop so that I might live, until, from loss to loss, nothing remains in me and my entire body falls beyond the limit—*cadre*, cadaver.[14]

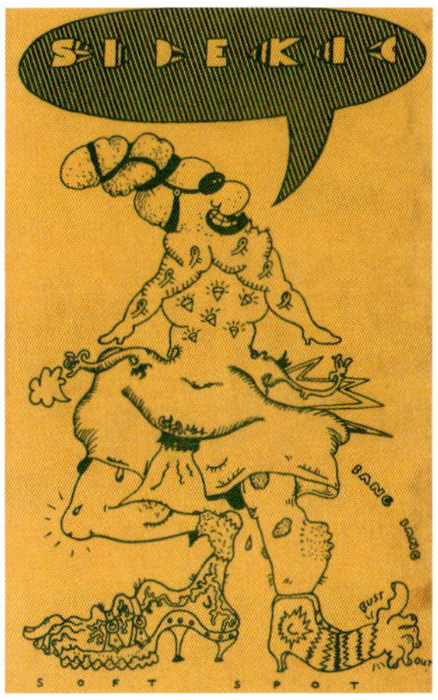

4.7 The Hairy Who, Cover of *The Hairy Who Sideshow*, 1967. Published for the second Hairy Who group exhibition at the Hyde Park Art Center, Chicago, February 24–March 24, 1967. Courtesy of the Roger Brown Study Collection, School of the Art Institute of Chicago.

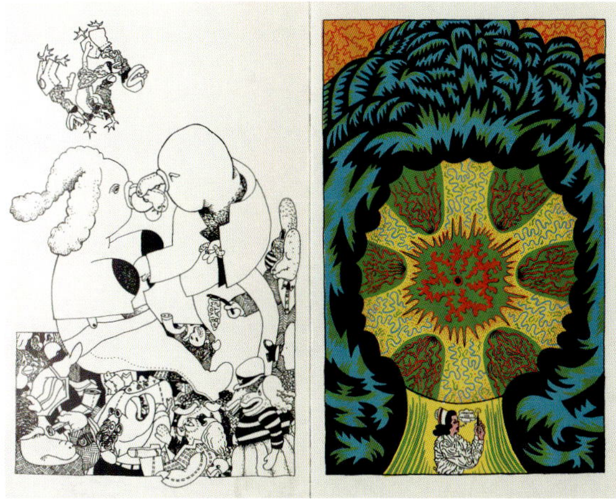

4.8 Gladys Nilsson (American, born 1940) and Karl Wirsum (American, born 1939). Page from *Hairy Who*, 1968, published for the third Hairy Who group exhibition at the Hyde Park Art Center, Chicago, April 5–May 11, 1968. Pennsylvania Academy of the Fine Arts, Philadelphia.

With Pop's excessive scrutiny of the means by which society communicated, self-presented, and addressed the challenges of being human and alive, there was little doubt that the abject would seep to the surface.

An abject approach to comic-book sources, celebrity, advertising, current events, and other Pop subjects is most consistently seen in the work of the artists who came together as the Hairy Who (1966–69)—Jim Falconer, Art Green, Gladys Nilsson, Jim Nutt, Suellen Rocca, and Karl Wirsum.[15] Their liberal disfiguration and reconfiguration of the body remains hilarious and repulsive, confidently unstable and admirably honest. In her seminal 1971 exhibition on the impact and use of comics in contemporary art, Joan Siegfield identified this in their work while paging through *The Hairy Who Sideshow* (**FIG. 4.7**), one of four comic books the group produced in conjunction with its exhibitions:

> The spectator is overwhelmed by the sight of fragmented images in a shapeless world. Figures are monstrously mutated, waving limbs like amputated stumps. They are beset by tongues and intestines, saliva, mucous, and excrement. . . . It is a vision of man reduced to his bodily functions, the kind of man American advertising struggles mightily to overcome with all its highly touted preparations for personal hygiene.[16]

The reader need not have made it to the interior of the comic to experience this cacophony of imaginative corporeal excess and mayhem. Describing what we witness as a "sideshow," the comic's title suggests living beings bearing physical aberrations that are fetishized in public out of fear and prurience. Works in the Hairy Who exhibitions carried these phantasms further. For instance, Art Green's *Absolute Purity* (1967) paired a flaming, putrescent, swollen, disembodied leg with a soft-serve ice-cream cone equal to it in height.

Gladys Nilsson's mass of aggressive, entangled, and overstimulated creatures—lizard-bird hybrids—which she contributed to one of the Hairy Who comics, show "movie stars" locked in a bite rather than a kiss (**FIG. 4.8**). Surrounding them are other creatures, staring, gawking, ogling, and bombarding them with salacious intrusion. On the adjacent page, Wirsum, as though playing directly off of this voyeurism and paparazzi pandemonium, presented an eye that aggressively hits the reader: entangled and frazzled wires of nerves and blood vessels squiggle away from the explosive center, and the entire (disembodied) organ swells toward the edges of the page like an expanding mushroom cloud. A nurse below prepares a numbing syringe. Both pages grew out of imagery that each artist was developing at the time, but the heightened aggression that is connected to "watching" and not being able to turn away feels further affected by contemporary media coverage of the Vietnam War.

Much of the work produced by the Hairy Who revels in the body on display without inhibitions. There is a willful confrontation with and embrace of its natural loathsomeness and desirability. Nutt's *Miss E. Knows* (**FIG. 4.9**), made with a sign painter's brush in reverse on Plexiglas, reveals these contradictory conditions—the adored body striving to attain "beauty" and the monstrous body that is in mortal disarray. Miss E.'s bubblegum-pink

4.9 Jim Nutt (American, born 1938). *Miss E. Knows*, 1967. Acrylic on Plexiglas with aluminum and rubber; enamel on wood frame; 75 ⅝ × 51 ⅝ in. The Art Institute of Chicago, Twentieth-Century Purchase Fund, 1970.1014.

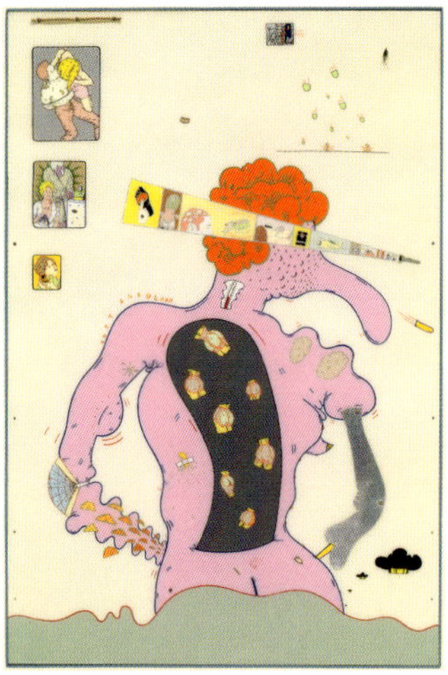

flesh swells and ripples as though it wanders independently of the body's underlying muscles. Her right arm ends abruptly in a stump that is connected to a prosthetic piece of aluminum that Nutt attached directly to the Plexiglas. Her nose is clongated grotesquely, suggesting a phallic protuberance that has affected the skin at its base so much that mouth and eyes have all but disappeared in a field of bumps and puckers.

Despite this condition, Miss E. poses coyly in the nude, sporting a shock of brilliant red hair and a sway to her hips that suggests she carries herself with confidence. Surrounding her and crossing over her face are compartmentalized illustrations, presenting motifs that include suspicious beauty treatments, extreme sexual practices, and voyeurism. If Nutt began with a pinup—and it is likely that he did—any trace of the source was reshaped through an imaginative and aggressive reconfiguration of the ads that bombard American women constantly with absurd messages about ideal beauty.[17]

Suellen Rocca's *Dream Girl* (cat. 36) is arranged around two central images—an eerily truncated torso that has "sausage curls" of hair rather than limbs (inspired by magazine advertisements of wigs and hairdos) and a green purse emblazoned with a shapely yellow leg.[18] Each is surrounded by a constellation of disembodied fingers, hands, and legs painted with a thin colored line, as well as images that promise paradise (tropical island), trophies, bunnies, and jewelry. Grabbing, touching, pointing, and caressing is everywhere in the painting, culminating with two outlines of female heads on pillows at the upper right and left bearing the words "Oh" and "Ah." *Dream Girl* seems to critique romantic expectations and the unrealistic demands that society places on women to attain its media-constructed picture of perfection.

Simply appropriating popular culture was never enough for Chicago artists; as far back as Albright, they subsumed it within their work and in doing so made objects and images that reveal as strong an obsession with the American vernacular as the work of their peers on the coasts. The Hairy Who and their contemporaries incorporated, and ultimately transformed, popular-culture imagery and mass-media techniques through an astute blending of advertising styles; Surrealism; designs and ritual objects from the Northwest Coast, Africa, and Polynesia; and a healthy dose of subjectivity. Pinball machines, reverse painting on windows done for mass production and for corner stores, childhood board games and toys, handmade signs, jewelry catalogues, bodybuilding and wrestling magazines, and neighborhood flyers and handbills excited them as much as (and perhaps more than) billboards, packaging, and television. Paschke emphasized this repeatedly, stressing that the local visual culture that sprang up on mass-produced posters and other printed matter appealed to him as much as the work of Warhol. He said, "For a while I was living in New York near Chinatown and here in Chicago in a Puerto Rican area, and various literatures that were strewn around the streets were things I found myself responding to out of a sort of grass roots sense of energy."[19] That desire to incorporate the local, the odd, and the unexpected with popular culture as a starting point gave Chicago art an edge that remains challenging and rewarding today.

ENDNOTES

1 For instance, see "Albright Twins: They Paint Gruesome Masterpieces in an Abandoned Methodist Church," *Life* (Mar. 27, 1944): 63–71; "Artist of Decay," *Newsweek* (Nov. 29, 1943): 82; "People Are Talking About . . . ," *Vogue* (Apr. 15, 1944): 98–99; and "U.S. Art: Albright," *Time* (July 6, 1942): 46–47.

2 For more on Albright's Hollywood projects, including extensive material from the Albert Lewin papers, see chapter four of Robert Cozzolino, "Every Picture Should Be a Prayer: The Art of Ivan Albright" (PhD diss., University of Wisconsin-Madison, 2006).

3 Alan G. Artner, "At 81, Ivan Albright Enjoys His Gift of Second Sight," *Chicago Tribune*, Oct. 22, 1978, 8.

4 Earle Ludgin to Ivan Albright, May 1, 1944, Ludgin Papers, Archives of American Art, Smithsonian Institution, Washington, D.C.

5 Critic Paul Richards recognized a link between Albright and a later generation: "Albright's paintings may well have influenced 'Tales from the Crypt' and the other creepy comic books that may well have influenced the Hairy Who." Paul Richard, "A 'Weird Coherent Vision': The Hairy Who," *Washington Post*, Apr. 20, 1969, 165.

6 For more on this issue, see Robert Cozzolino, *Art in Chicago: Resisting Regionalism, Transforming Modernism* (Philadelphia: Pennsylvania Academy of the Fine Arts, 2007).

7 Bruce Glaser, "Oldenburg, Lichtenstein, Warhol: A Discussion," *Artforum* (Feb. 1966): 20.

8 Claes Oldenburg, *Store Days: Documents from The Store (1961) and Ray Gun Theater (1962)* (New York: Something Else Press, 1967). "Statement" was originally published in 1961.

9 Russell Bowman, "An Interview with Roger Brown," *Art in America* 66, no. 1 (Jan.-Feb. 1978): 106–07.

10 Dan Nadel, "Hairy Who's History of Hairy Who," *The Ganzfeld* 3 (2003): 139–40.

11 Ellen H. Johnson, *Peter Saul* (New York: Allan Frumkin Gallery, 1964). Misperceptions that Saul was a Chicago artist date to at least 1962; Jack Kroll, "Peter Saul," *Art News* (Jan. 1962): 19.

12 This theme in Pop Art is largely unexamined. For a rare discussion of it, see Sidra Stich, *Made in USA: An Americanization in Modern Art, the '50s & '60s* (Berkeley: University Art Museum/University of California Press), 162–206. This is one of the few integrated, diverse studies of American Pop that also includes a strong selection of art by Chicagoans.

13 See *Peter Saul: New Paintings and Works on Paper* (New York: Allan Frumkin Gallery, 1987).

14 Julia Kristeva, *Powers of Horror: An Essay on Abjection* (New York: Columbia University Press, 1982), 3.

15 This abject quality affected one of the first critical commentators on the group, Franz Schulze, who consistently read them as provocateurs, delinquents, and adolescent mischief-makers obsessed with bodily fluids and sick jokes. Franz Schulze, "Chicago Popcycle," *Art in America* 54, no. 6 (Nov./Dec. 1966): 103–04; "Chicago," *Art International* 11, no. 5 (May 1967): 42–44.

16 Joan C. Siegfried, "Art from Comics," in *The Spirit of the Comics* (Philadelphia: Institute of Contemporary Art, University of Pennsylvania, 1971), n.p.

17 Jim Nutt, e-mail correspondence with the author, May 31, 2011.

18 Suellen Rocca, e-mail correspondence with the author, May 26, 2011.

19 Katherine Lee Keefe, "A Conversation [Don Baum, Roger Brown, Philip Hanson, Ed Paschke, Christina Ramberg, Barbara Rossi, and Ray Yoshida]," in *Some Recent Art from Chicago* (Chapel Hill: Ackland Art Museum, 1980), 33.

GERTRUDE ABERCROMBIE

Gertrude Abercrombie was a well-known figure in Chicago. She is remembered for her personal eccentricity; the salons she presided over at her Hyde Park row house, which attracted jazz musicians, writers, and visual artists; the regular spot she staked out at the Hyde Park Art Fair each year, with her old Rolls Royce parked nearby; and her completely distinctive imagery. Sometimes referred to as Surrealist or Magical Realist, it is in fact sui generis, her own vision and style.

Like many artists who remained in Chicago for the majority of their careers, Abercrombie followed her own path, developing away from the cultural dictates of the art centers on the East and West coasts. *Split Personality* treats themes she explored a number of times, with subtle variations. Here she included an image of herself in a barren room, with one of her possessions, a stoneware pitcher, placed strategically below her floating torso, as if she has risen, genielike, out of it. The image combines pathos and humor, alluding to the artist's feelings of dissociation and fragmentation, and her interest in magic, wordplay, and psychoanalysis. Much more interested in ideas than technique, she might have been describing this painting when she said, "Art has to be real 'crazy,' real personal and real real, or it is nowhere. If it doesn't make you laugh, it's not so good either."

SUSAN WEININGER

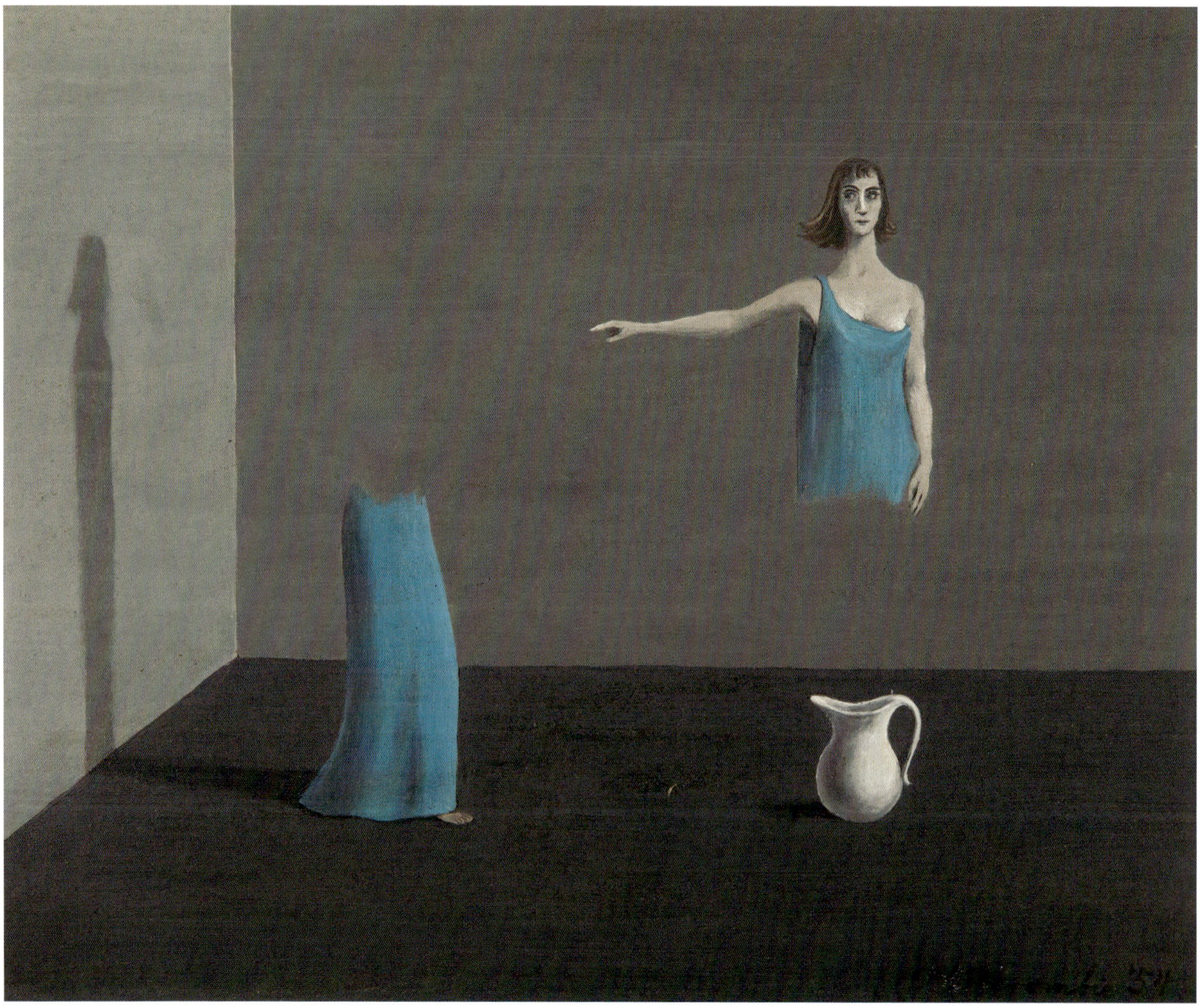

1. *Split Personality*, 1954
Oil on pressed board
Collection of the DePaul Art Museum, Art Acquisition Endowment, 2010.21

IVAN ALBRIGHT

When Ivan Albright painted this, his third documented self-portrait, he broke with the conventions of the genre by including no tangible references to his vocation as an artist. Instead, he depicted himself seated at a table in formal dress, cigarette held casually in his left hand while the fingertips of his other hand press against his cheek. With his calm demeanor and carefully considered pose and clothing, Albright presented a confident man who is as comfortable with his persona as with the materials and techniques of his trade.

Although modest in scale and made relatively early in his long career, the self-portrait emanates traces of Albright's evolving understanding of the duality of matter and spirit. It also proved to be critical to the development of relationships with influential patrons. After spotting the painting in an exhibition at the Art Institute, Chicago collector Earle Ludgin convinced Albright to make a second version. Similar in pose but substantially more intense in its degree of detail, the second version is like a doppelgänger of the first—the psychological dimension open to interpretation since Albright was a "mirror" twin to artist Malvin Marr Albright. This self-portrait was one of several paintings by Albright loaned to a high-profile touring exhibition in 1942–44, where film director Albert Lewin first saw the artist's work. He was so impressed that he commissioned Albright to paint *The Picture of Dorian Gray* (1943–44)(fig. 4.1) for his 1945 adaptation of the Oscar Wilde novel. By 1945 Albright had become the first internationally known Chicago artist.

ROBERT COZZOLINO

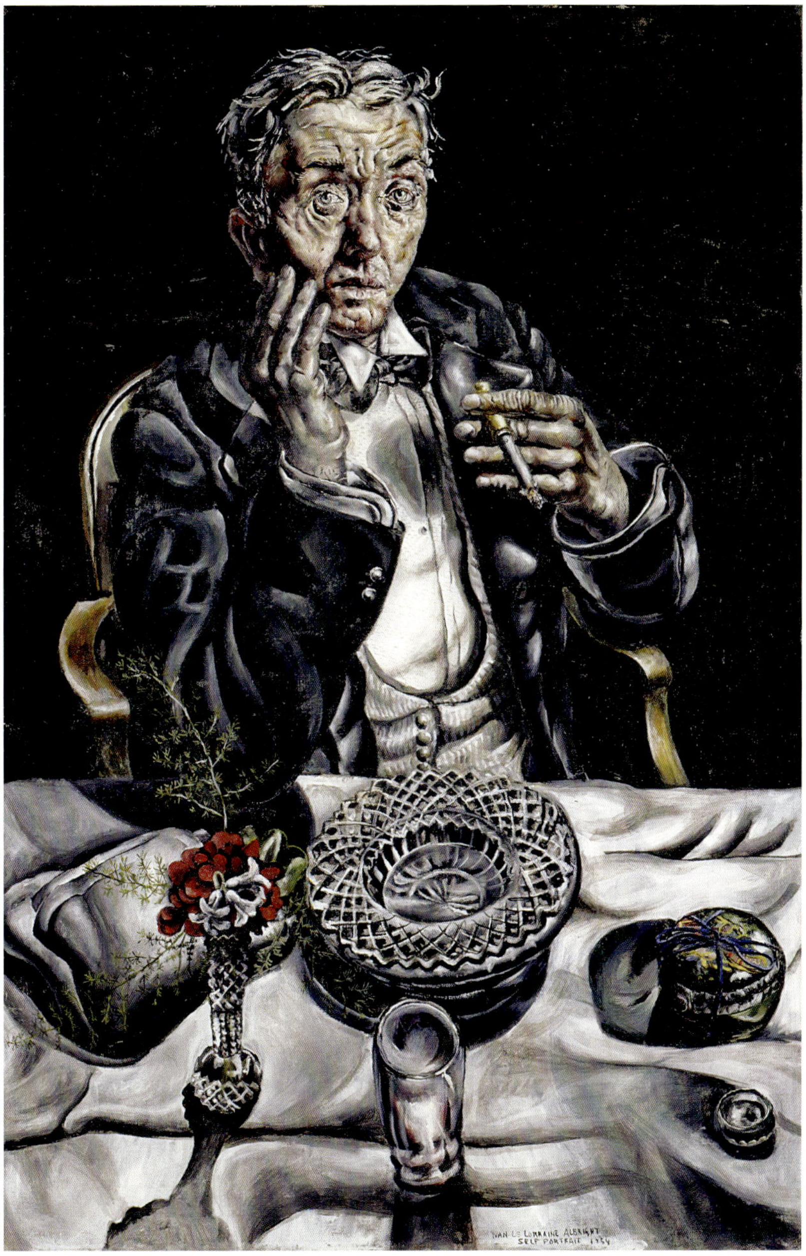

2. *Self-Portrait*, 1934
Oil on canvas
New Trier Township High School, District 203, Winnetka, Illinois

TIM ANDERSON

Tim Anderson is arguably one of the best portrait artists working today. For over three decades, he has focused almost exclusively on the human visage. His exploration of this enduring subject has led him into many areas of our culture and history, and his subjects form a pantheon of the famous and infamous, saints and sinners.

Anderson's oeuvre has appropriately focused on notable Chicago figures, from gangster icons like Al Capone to such literary giants as Nelson Algren and Studs Terkel. The painter Joan Mitchell, who was born in Chicago and educated at the School of the Art Institute of Chicago, is a subject very close to his heart. He has always loved her painting *City Landscape* (1955), which is in the collection of the Art Institute. What initially drew Anderson to this picture and ultimately to paint the artist was not only its painterly, expressive energy and bold scale but also Mitchell's exemplary biography. She was one of the few women Abstract Expressionists whose work rivaled that of her spiritual mentor, the legendary Abstract Expressionist pioneer Willem de Kooning.

Anderson's painting of Joan Mitchell is rendered in what has become his signature style: a large format (up to eight feet square) with a strong yellow background, and an extremely facile use of graphite that gives the composition subtlety and depth. Joan Mitchell is forever immortalized by Anderson's portrait, realized with loving commitment and consummate skill.

COREY POSTIGLIONE

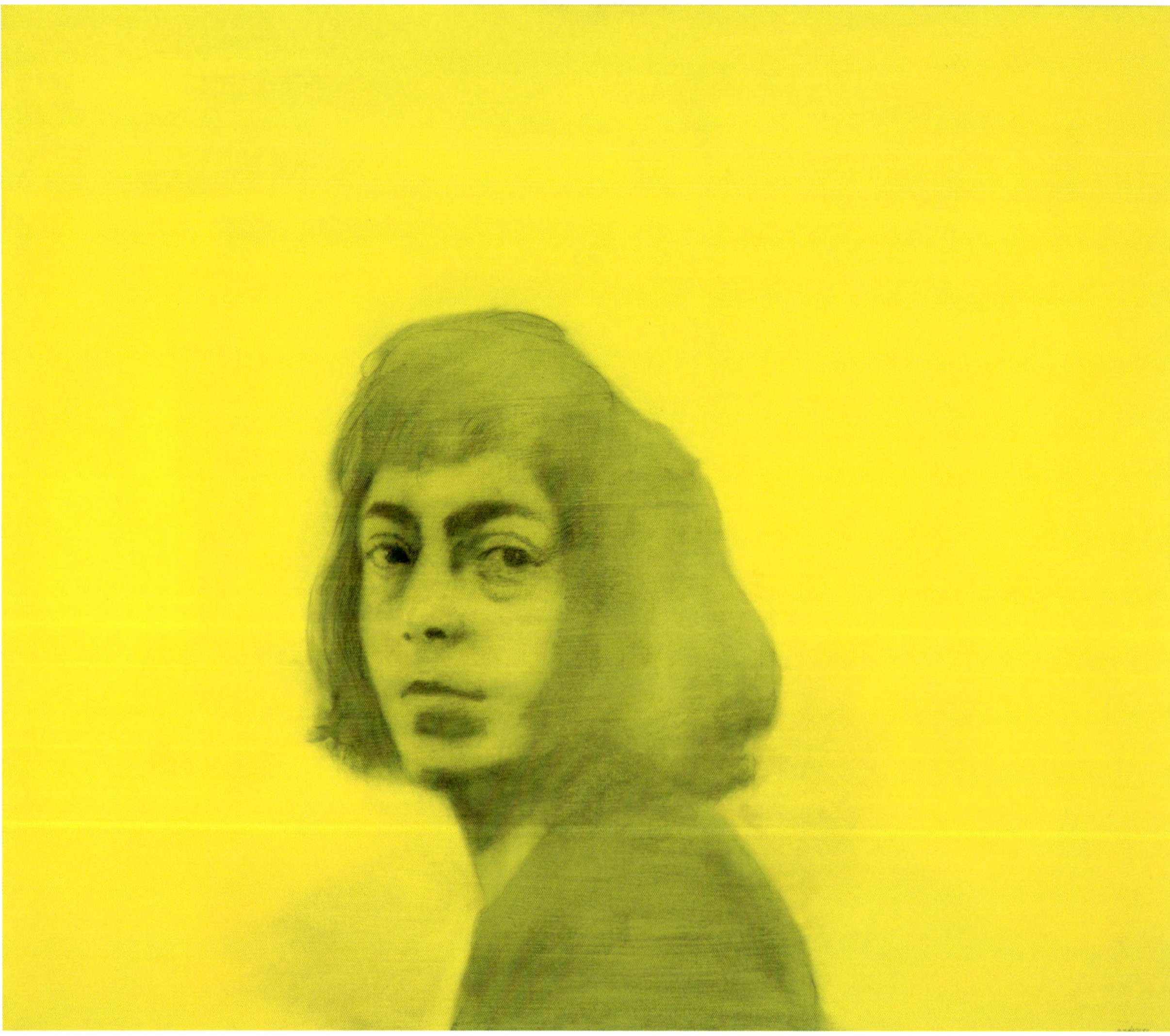

3. *AB-EX*, 2008
Oil and graphite on canvas
Collection of the artist

RALPH ARNOLD

Ralph Arnold grew up in South Chicago and went on to study art at the University of Illinois and Roosevelt University; he ultimately received a master of fine arts from the School of the Art Institute of Chicago. Thereafter, he balanced a professional life as a teacher at Barat College and Loyola University in Chicago with his artistic practice, which encompassed painting, printmaking, and—perhaps most strikingly—collage.

By all accounts, Arnold moved in a number of communities with considerable ease but little attachment—from academic art circles to the Southside gang neighborhood where he taught painting. *Who You/Yeah Baby* is a prime example of his mixed-media work: an assortment of men's fashion images are held in tension by strongly colored background stripes and culminate in the matching gestures of Uncle Sam and a model in a plaid suit. The stenciled title seems to allude to the role of clothing in self-presentation; only the presence of Uncle Sam, associated at the time with military recruiting for the unpopular Vietnam War, hints at the turbulent events of 1968, when this painting was likely made. Arnold's politics, like his attitudes toward issues of race and sexual identity, are presented with subtlety and a degree of irony.

DARBY ENGLISH
(TEXT BY LOUISE LINCOLN)

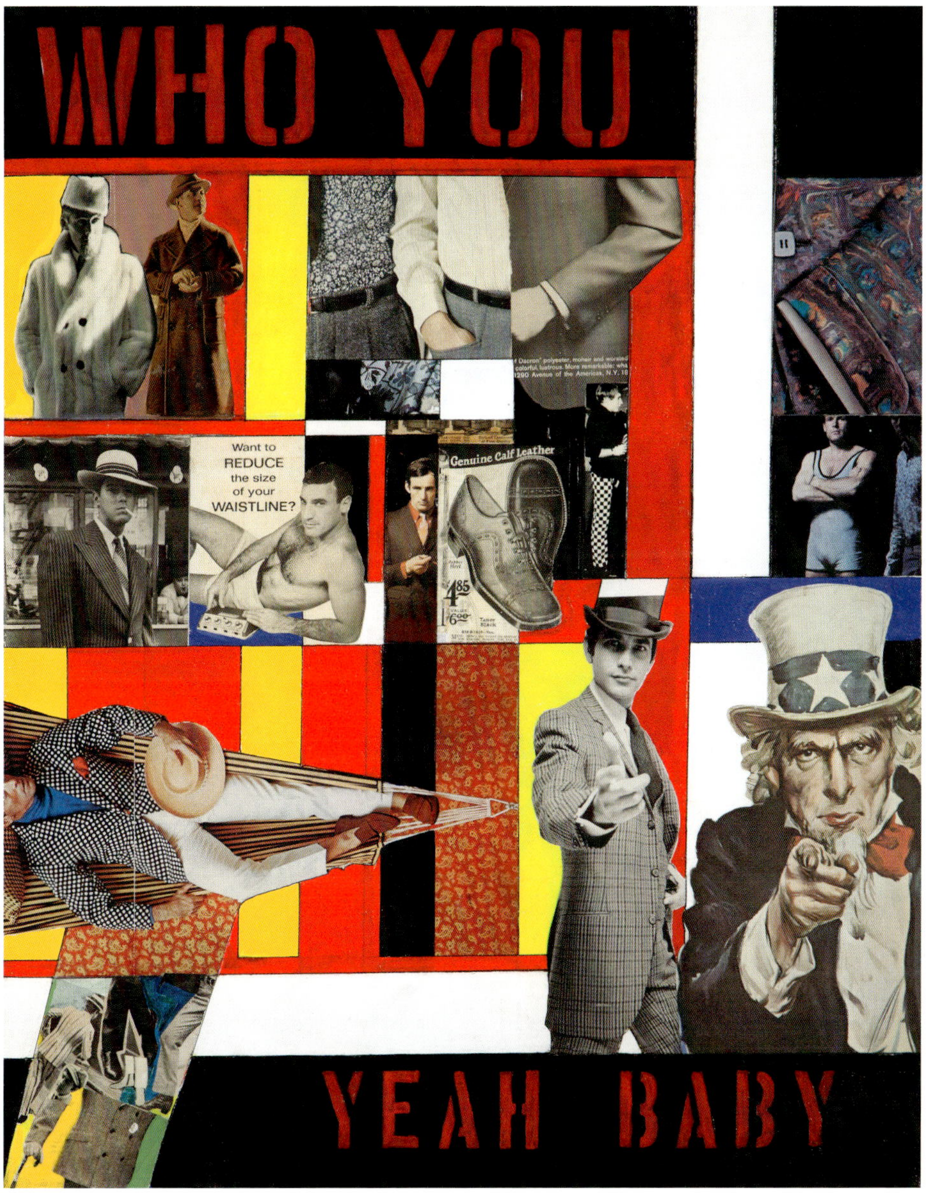

4. *Who You/Yeah Baby*, c. 1968
Oil and collage on canvas
Collection of the DePaul Art Museum,
Art Acquisition Endowment, 2008.81

MACENA BARTON

Macena Barton hardly fits any artistic category, and as a result has been largely excluded from conventional art history. Although she practiced in the traditional genre of portraiture, she paradoxically used costumes, props, and vivid colors to indicate an ideological understanding of gender roles and culture as performative. Her nudes and self-portraits follow this same formula: she often significantly altered her appearance, suggesting a socially constructed identity. The issues Barton and her female colleagues commented upon informed the artistic alliances they later created in order to combat sexism. Many of these coalitions, such as the Women Artists' Salon of Chicago, grew out of their association with the Federal Arts Project of the New Deal. Although women artists were welcomed into the relatively egalitarian Works Progress Administration, stigmas haunt women artists even now.

Barton surrounded her subjects with decorative auras during the 1930s, but abruptly stopped producing these devices when they drew critical praise. This act of defiance exemplifies her reluctance to be categorized. Here she countered the male gaze while presenting a chiseled and forward, yet soft and vulnerable body position. Hard geometric shapes delicately balance the entire composition. Everything within this canvas fits, but upon closer view is contradictory, a fitting description of the artist herself. Barton continued to record herself ambiguously, often using culturally charged imagery, until her death.

JAMIE SHAW

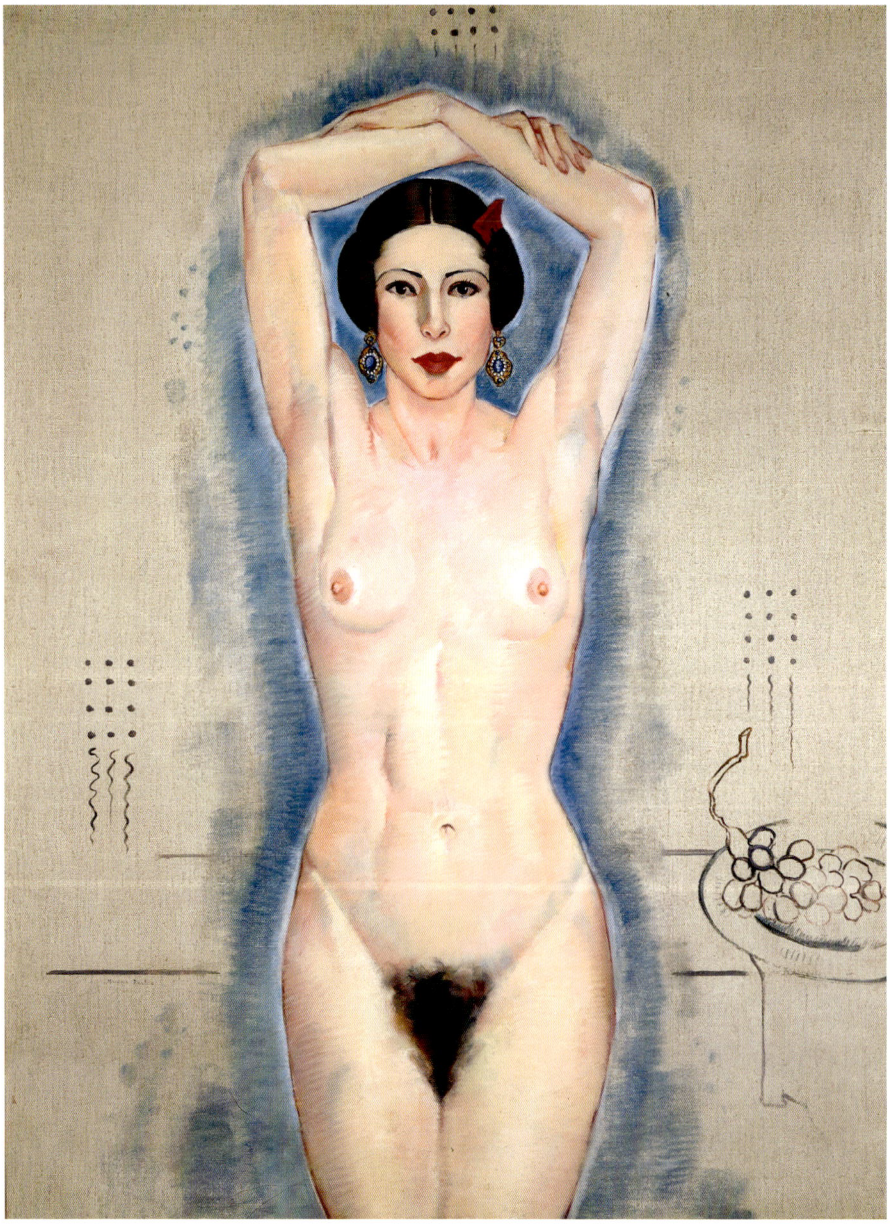

5. *Self-Portrait*, c. 1932
Oil on canvas
Collection of Mr. and Mrs. Harlan J. Berk

DON BAUM

Don Baum was an assemblage artist first and foremost, working the detritus of the vernacular into bristly sculptures and friezes that tweaked the ponderous and pretentious in art history. Around 1979, influenced by a book about medieval peasant life, he began a series of house-shaped sculptures. Utterly simple in form, these explorations of primordial shelter were covered with exuberant collages of travel brochures and copies of Renaissance murals mixed with scraps of old paintings, wallpaper, game boards, and whatever else he could scrounge up in junk shops. In *ARF* the homey images of paint-by-number hunting scenes and landscapes are somehow harmonized with a painting of the Last Supper, bringing together the subjects of sustenance, humans (and dogs) in nature, and a glimpse of another world.

Baum was also a teacher and a frequent guest curator at the Hyde Park Art Center, and his assemblage technique surely relates to his curatorial practice. He was a champion of Chicago artists and the catalyst for early shows of the Hairy Who and other outrageously anti-canonical groups of the late 1960s. Selecting promising but disparate pieces and bringing them into an unexpected and startling juxtaposition, he created exhibitions that, like his sculptures, were provocative, revelatory, and frequently hilarious.

LOUISE LINCOLN

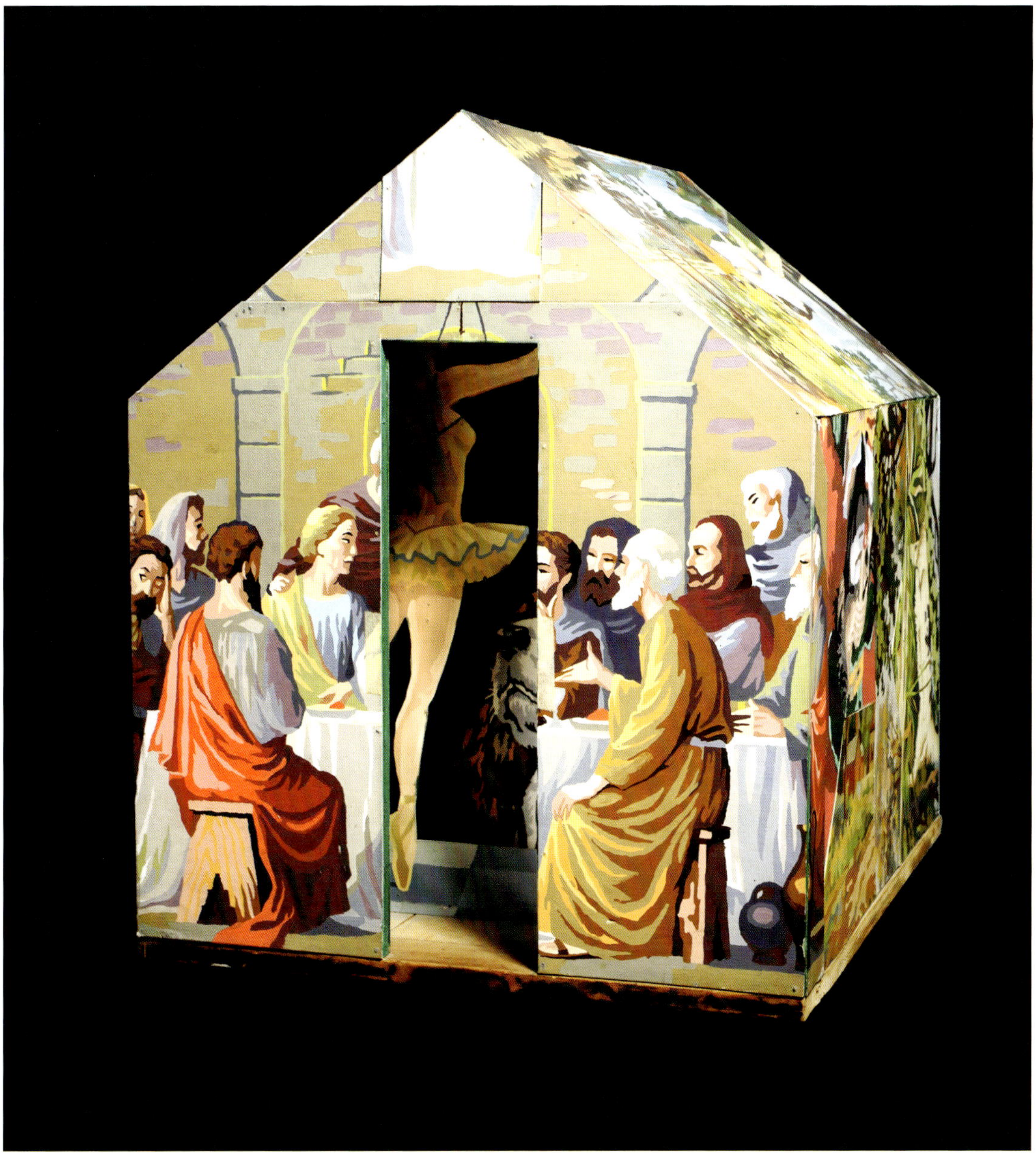

6. *ARF*, 1986
Mixed-media sculpture
Estate of Don Baum, courtesy of
Carl Hammer Gallery

MARIE KRANE BERGMAN AND CREAM CO.

Marie Krane Bergman creates paintings that seem to be monochrome abstractions, but are actually made up of thousands of perfectly shaped gridded ovals of paint. The little ovals seem to be the same hue, but as you look, the composition changes color from one side to the other. This gradual shift is actually a meticulous, ultrarealist record of the incremental color alterations of flowers from Bergman's garden as they fade and dry.

Bergman's process is so time-consuming that she collaborates with others to execute her paintings and collectively credits them to Cream Co. This working method is analogous to that of the workshops run by premodern painters, and it makes the experience of viewing her canvases that much richer. This site-specific collage brings the collaborative aspects of Cream Co. to the fore. Here Bergman and her collaborators dripped paint, left over from countless attempts at recording particular slices of time, down threads suspended from the ceiling. When the threads dried, Bergman precisely sequenced them in a nearly imperceptible reduction of color. The installation bears the same relationship to the accompanying painting as the painting does to the flower: it is a nuanced transcription of time, change, and representation.

Bergman and Cream Co.'s practice is balanced between abstraction and hyperrealism, Conceptualism and Romanticism, Minimalism and representation, temporality and instantaneity, pattern and process, auteur work and collaboration, and success and failure.

JAMES ELKINS

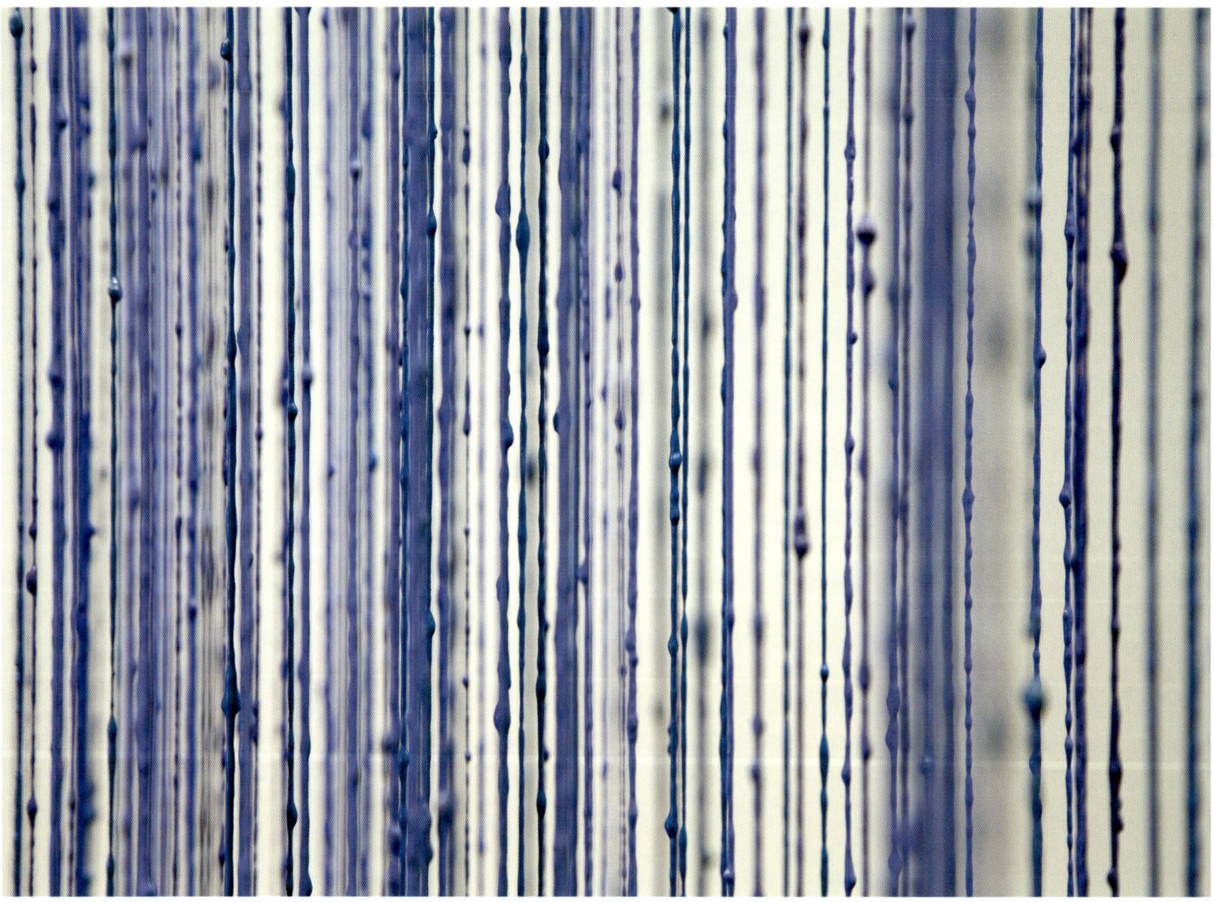

7. *Years, Years Later, in Weeks*, 2011
Acrylic on thread, paperclips, and shadows
Courtesy of Cream Co.

DAWOUD BEY

In 2001 Dawoud Bey had some time to himself. It was summer, and the classes he taught at Columbia College were over. He stepped out of his apartment building and into the park directly across the street. Not since his earliest days as a photographer working in black and white had he roamed around making street portraits. Now he worked in color but continued to use a four-by-five-inch view camera, which required a deliberate dedication to equipment and posing his subjects.

His own bold work of multiple, large-scale color Polaroid portraits had given way to a new, but more traditional approach of single-framed studio portraits. And likely there were a thousand other unaccountable things calling for his attention. Mostly there was fresh air, the squawk of Hyde Park's wild green parrots, picnickers, elderly bench sitters, tennis players, and, of course, a healthy spectrum of children. Bey set up his tripod and camera in the park, often just letting his subjects come to him. One after another, sitters found the photographer or vice versa, and one after another, sensitive portraits resulted.

One of the artist's chance encounters was with Muhammad, whose family had come to Chicago's Southside from Africa. Muhammad was a bright boy of about ten who spoke Arabic, French, English, and probably four or five African languages. He posed willingly with his bicycle, revealing the trusting, pensive face that Bey is able to coax masterfully from carefree, wondering grade-schoolers and moody, self-obsessed high-school students.

DAVID TRAVIS

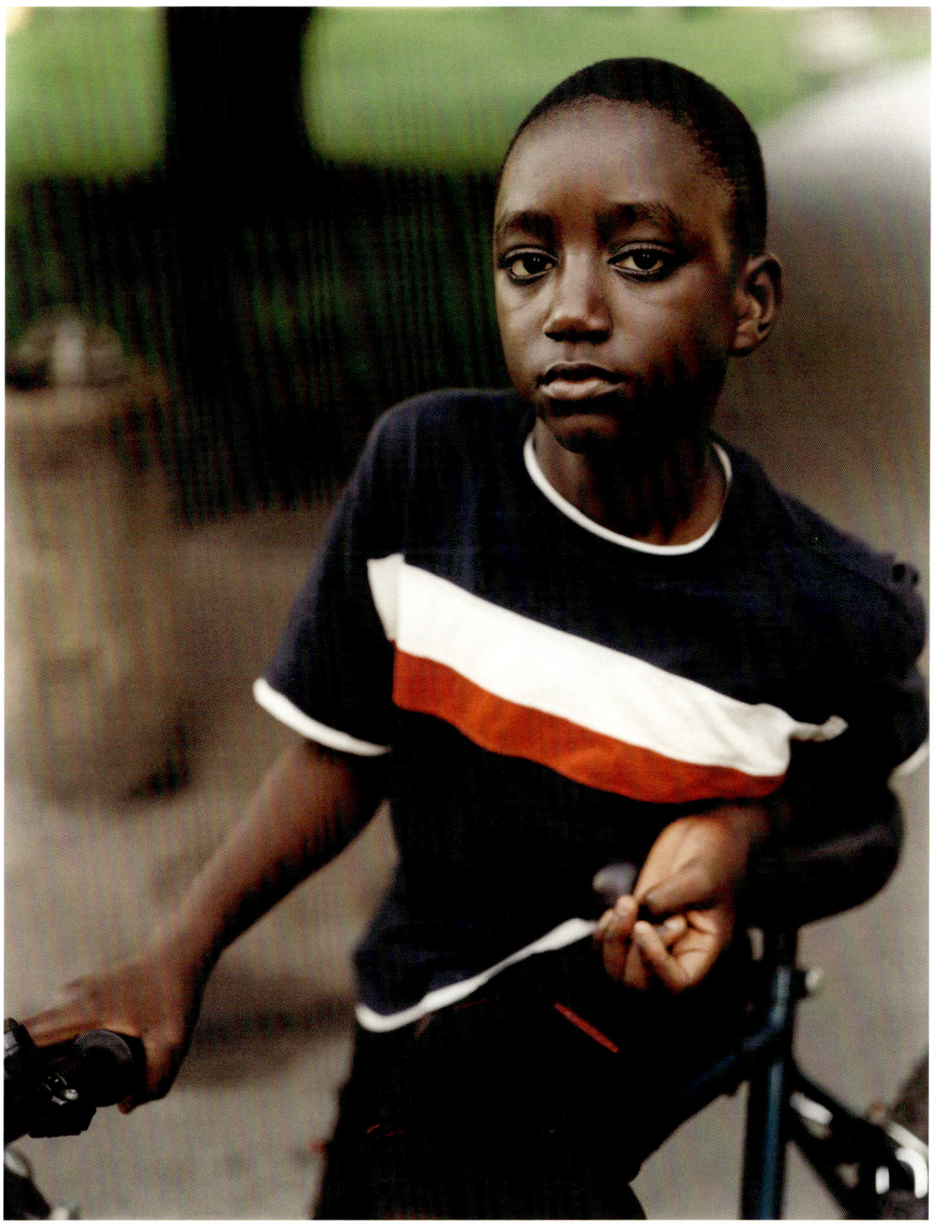

8. *Muhammad (Chicago)*, 2001
Archival pigment print
Collection of the DePaul Art Museum,
Art Aquisition Endowment, 2011.13

MARGARET BURROUGHS

Margaret Burroughs is remembered by the Chicago arts community as a founder of the DuSable Museum of African American History and the South Side Community Art Center, as a poet, and as a scholar of African American culture. These significant accomplishments often eclipse her production in the visual arts, but Burroughs was also an accomplished painter, draftsman, and printmaker. Utilizing figuration in dialogue with African traditions, social realism, and European modernism, her images encourage the viewer to engage with the history and iconic voices of the Abolitionist and Civil Rights movements. More subtle, but equally powerful, are Burroughs's images of ordinary and tender moments in the African American community—a family sharing a meal, the embrace of a mother and child, a girl playing hopscotch or sitting in front of a classroom—which suggest the promise of racial equality for succeeding generations.

Peace features two girls, one African American and one white. The former stares outward with her black and white cat. The latter offers a red bird, an acknowledgment of the blood shed due to racism, yet also a commitment to an integrated future. The cat's disinterest in the bird may be read as an acceptance of her offering and a common desire to move forward in peace.

JOANNA GARDNER-HUGGETT

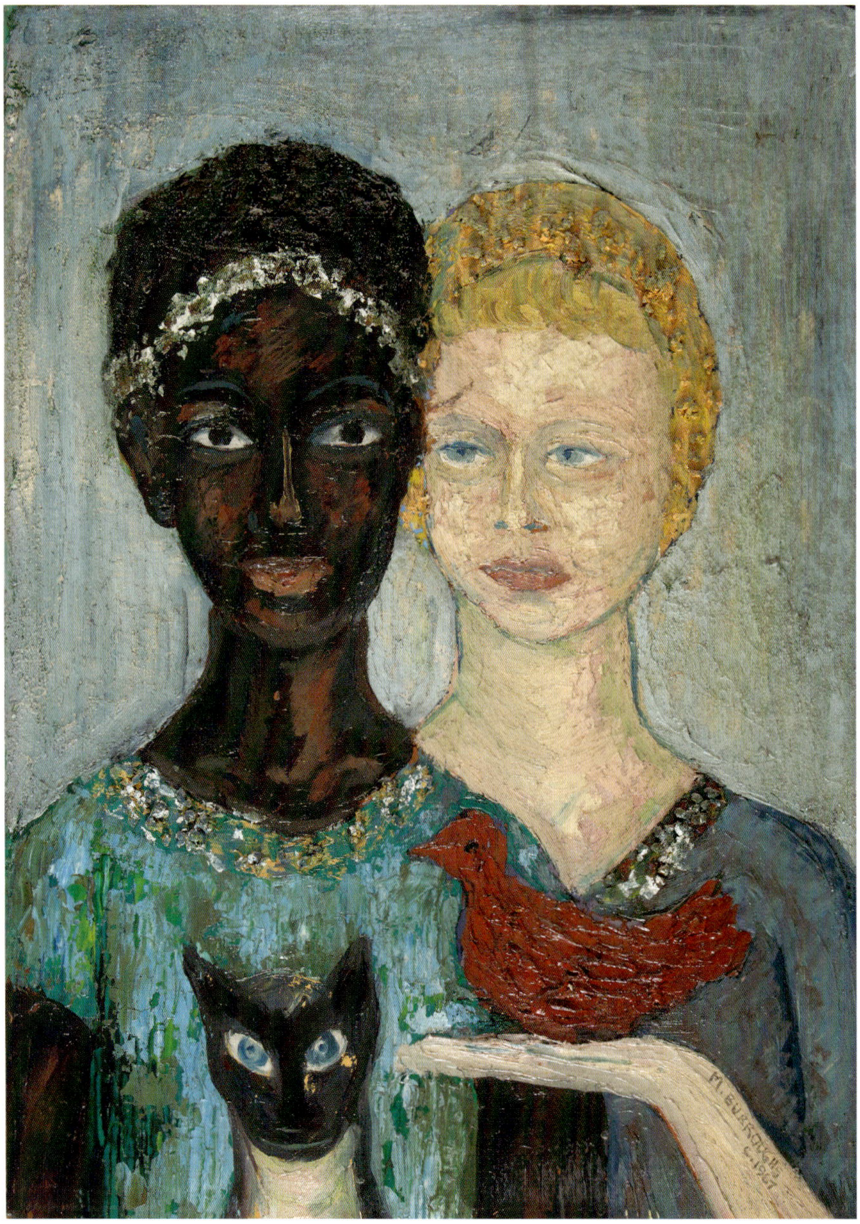

9. *Peace*, 1967
Oil on Masonite
Collection of Shay and Christopher Brokemond

HARRY CALLAHAN

I met Harry Callahan once. I have met a lot of important, even legendary, figures and know some of them well. Such artists are not for me denizens of some mythic universe I wish I could inhabit. But I did feel this way about Callahan, and it was a high point in my life to meet him, have dinner with him, and meet his—equally for me—legendary wife and muse, Eleanor. To me Callahan is a giant, yet here in Chicago, people outside the photography community barely know of him.

Callahan was near the end of his life and having difficulty swallowing when I met him. So while we all ate dinner, he sat and did not eat or say much. But he was alert and attentive. Extraordinary happiness shaped his still-handsome face, and there was a radiant twinkle in his eye—that eye that looked through so many viewfinders to capture some of the twentieth century's most iconic images.

This photograph, showing two pedestrians—one male, one female—passing on a Chicago bridge in 1960, stands among Callahan's best, and a more ravishing composition can hardly be imagined. Yet the subject matter is completely quotidian: two people walking in the city. It is but one of many, many such astonishing works of art that Callahan captured with his fine-tuned sense of vision, an extraordinary gift he gave to the world but especially to all of us who call ourselves Chicagoans.

LYNNE WARREN

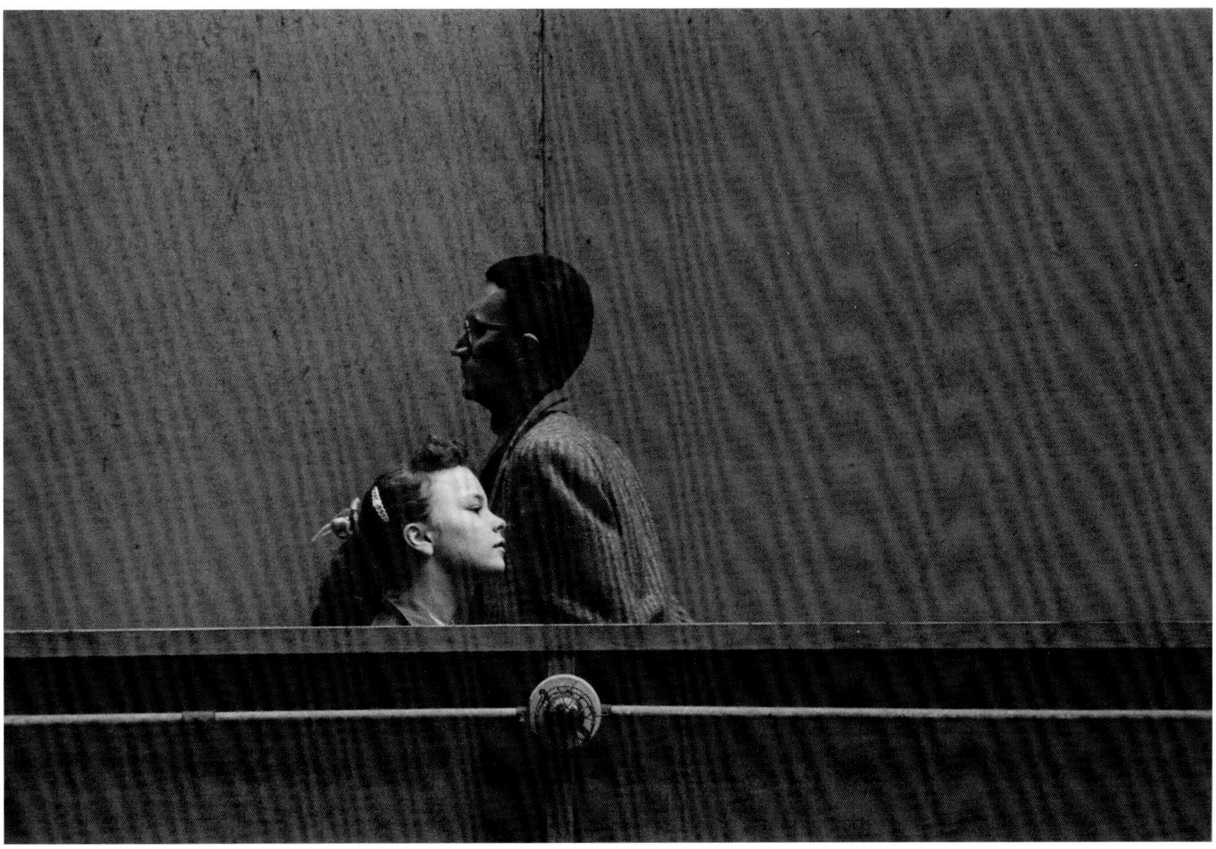

10. *Untitled*, 1960
Gelatin silver print
Collection of the DePaul Art Museum,
Art Acquisition Endowment, 2003.15

NICK CAVE

Some clothes we wear to be invisible, to blend in; other clothes extend our personhood and beg passersby for interface. Nick Cave's *Soundsuits* are neither office casual nor black tie. They belong to a special category of dress reserved for transforming everyday realities into celebrations, holy days, pageants, carnivals, and rituals. But which rituals? Who wears this cloak? Cave's *Soundsuits* need not be linked to a particular magical or spiritual tradition. In fact, it is their upending and blending of diverse cultural references that make them best suited to outfitting our formless fears and dreams.

Each Halloween, for just one night, we celebrate the gruesomeness of death and decay, perhaps to reflect on the growth of life and love, and to explore the possibility of changeable identities. Likewise, the *Soundsuits* ask, what if every day is a ritual? Could our everyday clothes incite us to embrace the strange? This *Soundsuit* is unworn, unanimated. It can be admired for its craftsmanship and energized aesthetics, but like a dress hanging in your closet, it awaits your choice of who or what you will be today. It is amazing what you can get away with when wearing a costume.

JASON FOUMBERG

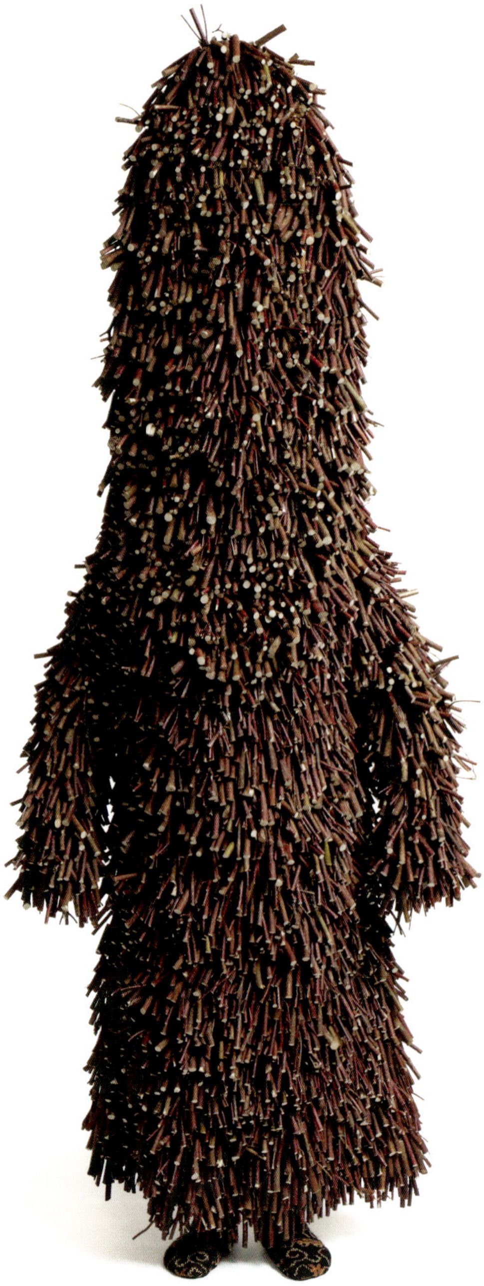

11. *Soundsuit*, 2010
Mixed media
Courtesy of Jack Shainman Gallery, New York

JUAN ANGEL CHAVEZ

I remember encountering Juan Chavez's work for the first time on the corner of Damen and Chicago avenues in the early 1990s. A primary-colored Constructivist sculpture, made from found wood and plastic, brightened up the entrance of an abandoned building in the once-edgy West Town. I'd seen that work frequently for years, until someone decided to steal it. In those days, you had to experience Urban Art in situ, since there were no blogs or Web sites to document the street-art scene. You would stumble upon a work accidentally or find yourself navigating unknown streets just to catch a glimpse of what your friends told you was on the corner of this and that. It was a great strategy to distribute ideas, and Chavez was among the first to use this approach to beautify our public spaces.

Although Chavez is an expert artisan, it is his works that assemble the detritus of our society that are the most compelling. I love his pieces created out of materials found in dumpsters or carpenter shops, often plain old junk he picked up on the street and hauled away in his pickup truck. *No Campground Just Water* is a perfect example of the controlled chaos of the artist's reusable craft. The sculpture looks like a crash-landed meteor or space capsule made from wood, cloth, canvas, plastic, trash, and even some stuffed animals. A metaphor for Chavez's experience growing up in the United States—gathering language, stories, and awareness as he navigated new society—the piece speaks to the nature of immigrant adaptability and resourcefulness.

ED MARSZEWSKI

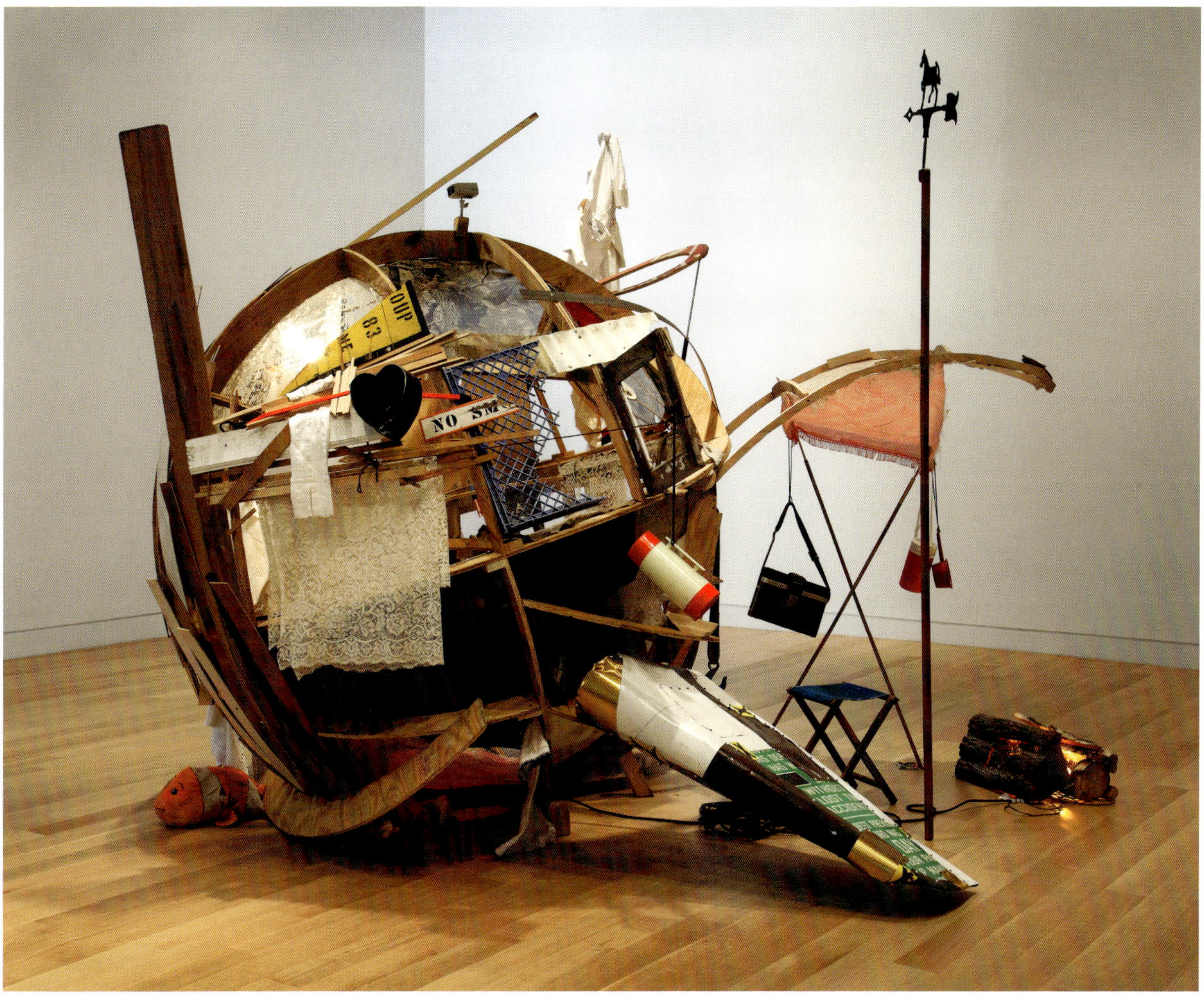

12. *No Campground Just Water*, c. 2005
Found objects and plywood
Collection of the artist

WILLIAM CONGER

A common thread that runs through this exhibition and catalogue involves the Hairy Who and its legacy. Playful, colorful, perverse, and irreverent, the artists involved with this down-home Chicago art movement made certain that their work was distinct and unique. At first glance Bill Conger's *Gemini* may not seem to have much in common with the typically figurative work of the Hairy Who, but this painting is more snag than easy weave.

The forms, marks, and surfaces in *Gemini* suggest associations with New York School abstraction but in total the work betrays other allegiances. These involve formal approaches and thematic attitudes consistent with Chicago image makers. For example, the highly keyed colors of *Gemini* are at odds with the New York school of abstraction. Particular forms glint in an artificial light within the painting. These forms suggest volumes in a space and therefore distinguish themselves from the painted traces and process residues of the particular mid-Atlantic regionalism championed by the critic Clement Greenberg. Surely this is not the abstraction of our forebears.

This work is playful, colorful, perverse and irreverent. With pitch-perfect Hairy Who attitude, *Gemini* is a tangled knot in the warp and weft of twentieth-century American art.

MATTHEW GIRSON

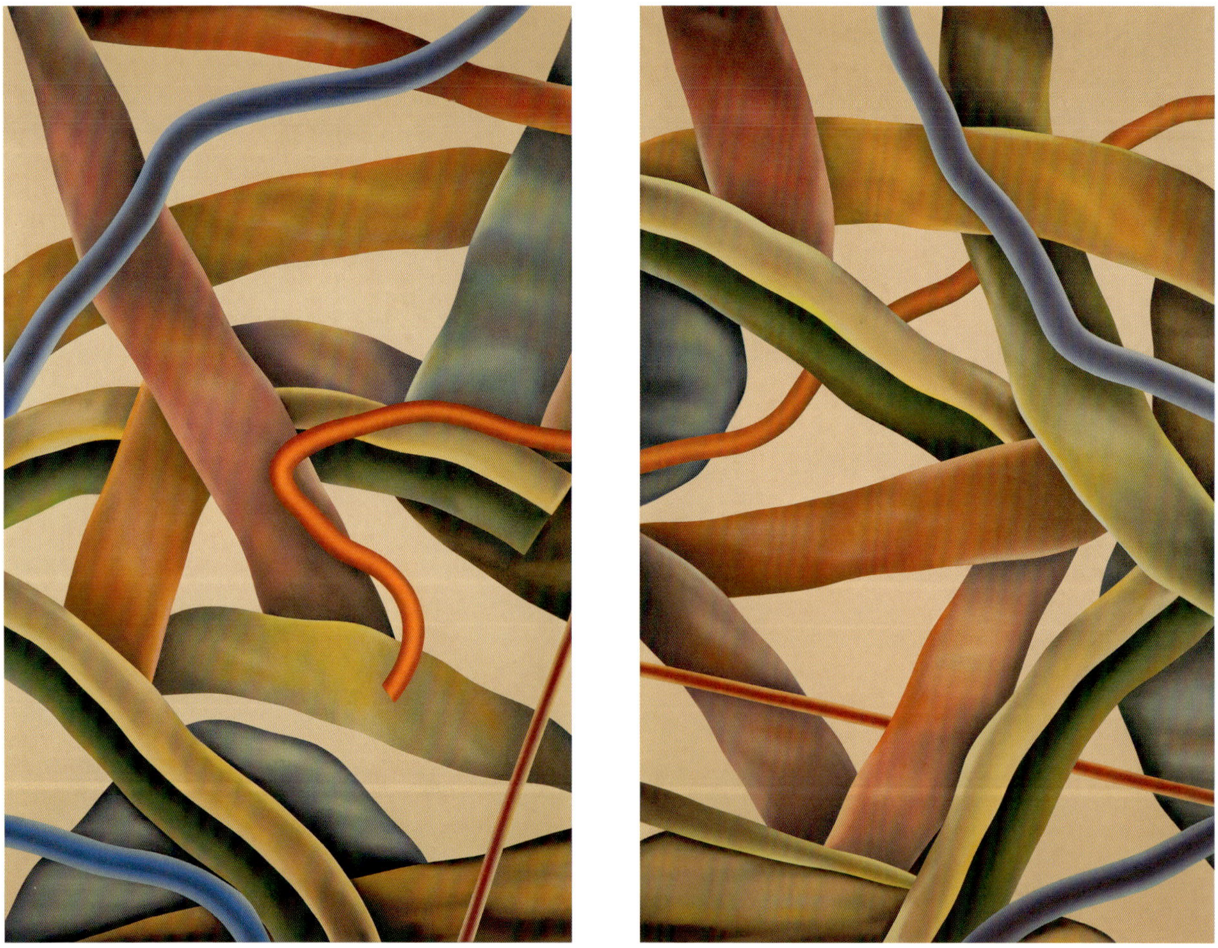

13. *Gemini* (diptych), 1974
Oil on canvas
Collection of the DePaul Art Museum,
gift of Mary and John Gedo, 2008.76–77

PAUL D'AMATO

Paul D'Amato's photographs are insistent. They implore you to look and to question how you see. Photography is a notoriously slippery medium for such a task, but how the photographer navigates that terrain is often what makes the images compelling. At its core, D'Amato's work grapples with the limitations of photography to convey a narrative or express a definitive fact. How does a photographer, an artist, reconcile the opposing truths that every photograph is at once a fabrication, and a representation of someone or something that does in fact inhabit the real world?

Though he may not have the answers, D'Amato does not dodge this quandary. For the past twenty-some years, he has chronicled the lives of ordinary Chicagoans in a way that could best be described as "creative nonfiction." D'Amato spends many years photographing a community to deepen his relationships to his subjects and to try to overcome the tropes of traditional documentary photographs. In 2003 he began photographing in Chicago's public-housing projects, among them Cabrini-Green along Division Street, where this photograph was made. D'Amato's vivid visual prose, describing a concrete tower in the midst of demolition, simultaneously evokes stories of a cherished home, a bonded community, and the ruins of social and political idealism gone awry. The narratives contained in this image, though rich in detail and fraught with emotion, are ultimately and intentionally ambivalent and far from complete.

GREGORY J. HARRIS

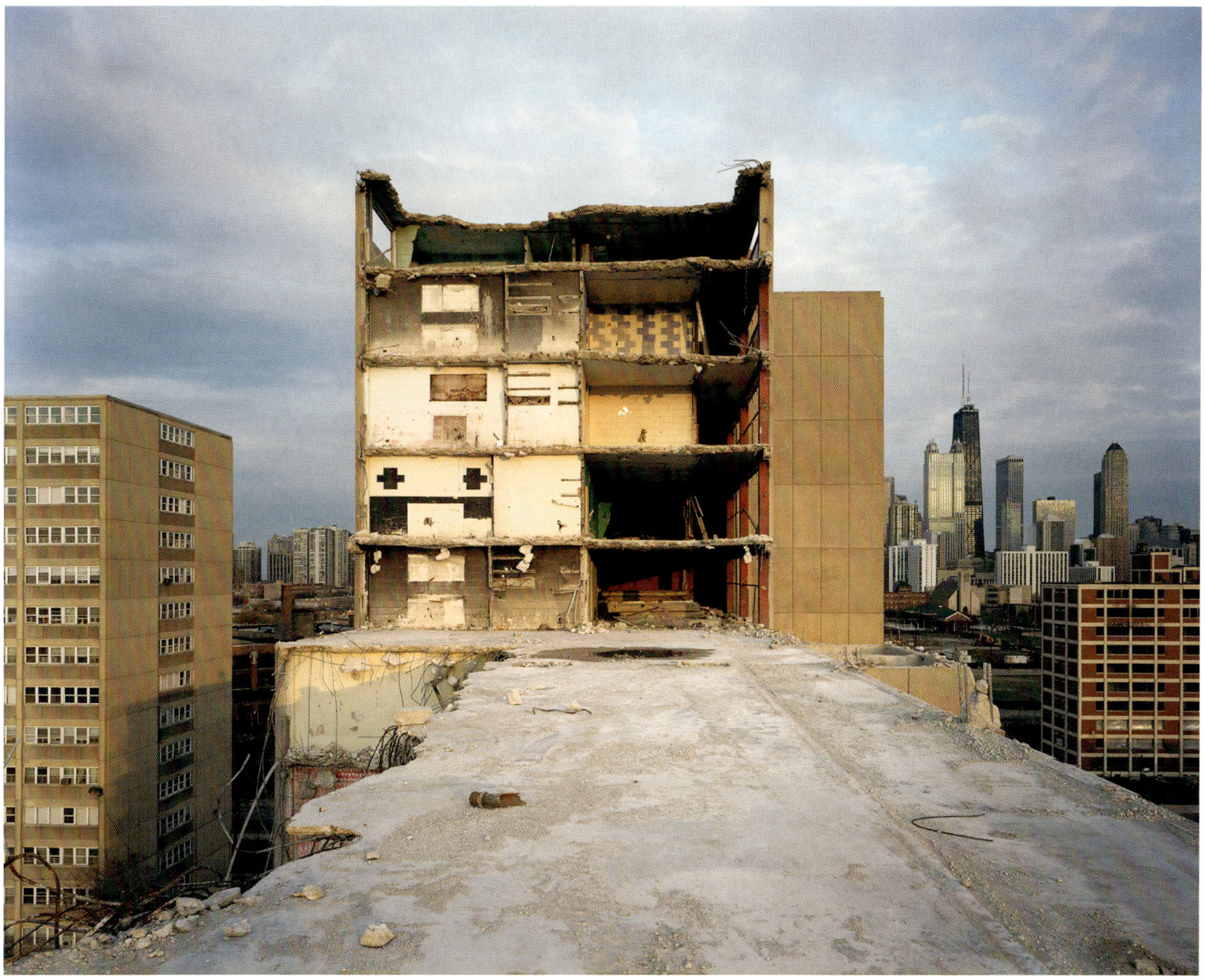

14. *634 W. Division, Chicago*, 2007
Archival pigment print
Collection of the DePaul Art Museum,
Art Acquisition Endowment, 2010.69

HENRY DARGER

Henry Darger was anything but famous during his lifetime. The devout Catholic lived a humble life in a small Lincoln Park apartment at the edge of the DePaul University campus. Yet after his death, his landlord, Nathan Lerner, discovered that Darger had produced a large body of creative work. He had written two epic novels about the struggles of seven girls (the Vivian sisters) against armies of evil men and made hundreds of corresponding illustrations. These works range from small drawings and tracings to elaborate ten-foot-long paintings. Though his life seemed quite modest, Darger was, in fact, a complex and prolific artist.

Darger's art illustrates a fantastic narrative, but its imagery is rooted in the everyday experience of visual culture in Chicago. Having never studied art formally, he developed his own technique for tracing and collaging imagery from mass print sources, including comics, magazines, newspapers, and coloring books. In *2 at Cedernine . . . / 15 at Battle of Norma Catherine*, for example, Darger traced images of girls from coloring books and advertisements and collaged newsprint figures of soldiers, birds, a hot-air balloon, and bits of landscape. Embedding this ordinary print media into his imaginative battlefield scene, the artist presented a fascinating mix of personal fantasy and popular culture.

MARY TRENT

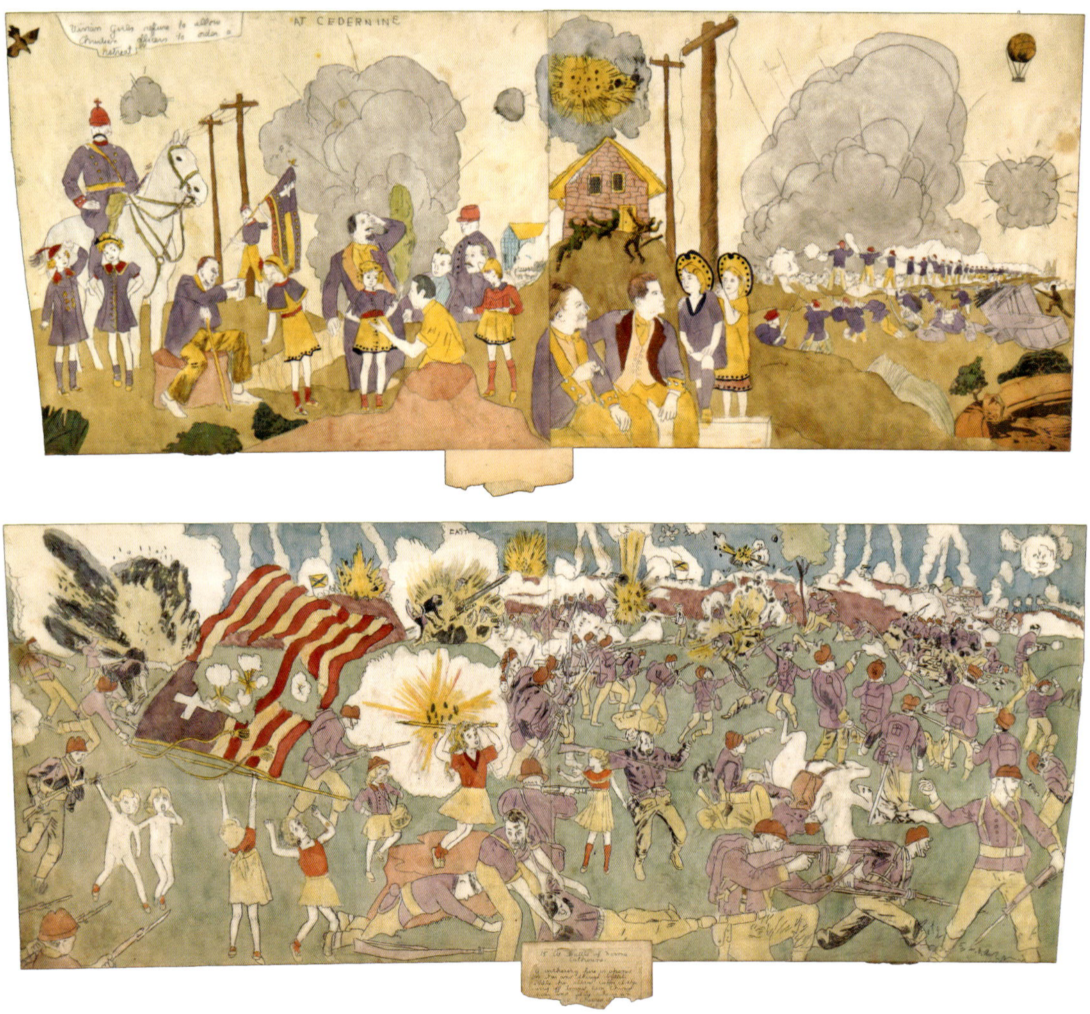

15. *2 at Cedernine . . . /15 at Battle of Norma Catherine*, n.d.
Watercolor and graphite on paper
Collection of Bob Roth

ARTHUR B. DAVIES

Arthur B. Davies was born in Utica, New York, but in 1878 his family moved to Chicago, where he attended the Chicago Academy of Design. He was a member of The Eight, a group of artists known for their gritty Ashcan realism, but his ethereal figures and idealized landscapes are more closely aligned with the European traditions in which he found inspiration: the Symbolism of Pierre Puvis de Chavannes, the Romanticism of the Pre-Raphaelites, and the Classicism of the Italian Renaissance. Collector Duncan Phillips once called him "the unicorn of modern painting."

Davies is best known for his role in introducing European modernism to the United States, as the president of the American Association of Painters and Sculptors, which organized the Armory Show in 1913. Davies was widely collected in his day, and *Helen, the Dawn Flower* was originally part of the collection of the Art Institute, bequeathed in 1933 by one of its founding trustees, Martin A. Ryerson. The artist's inscription of a passage by the Spanish Baroque poet Lope de Vega on the painting's stretcher, as well as the composition's lush color and classical figure, pay homage to his European influences. But the nude placed in front of a partly drawn curtain presents a witty twist on *Venus Rising from the Sea* by the American artist Raphaelle Peale.

KIRSTEN M. JENSEN

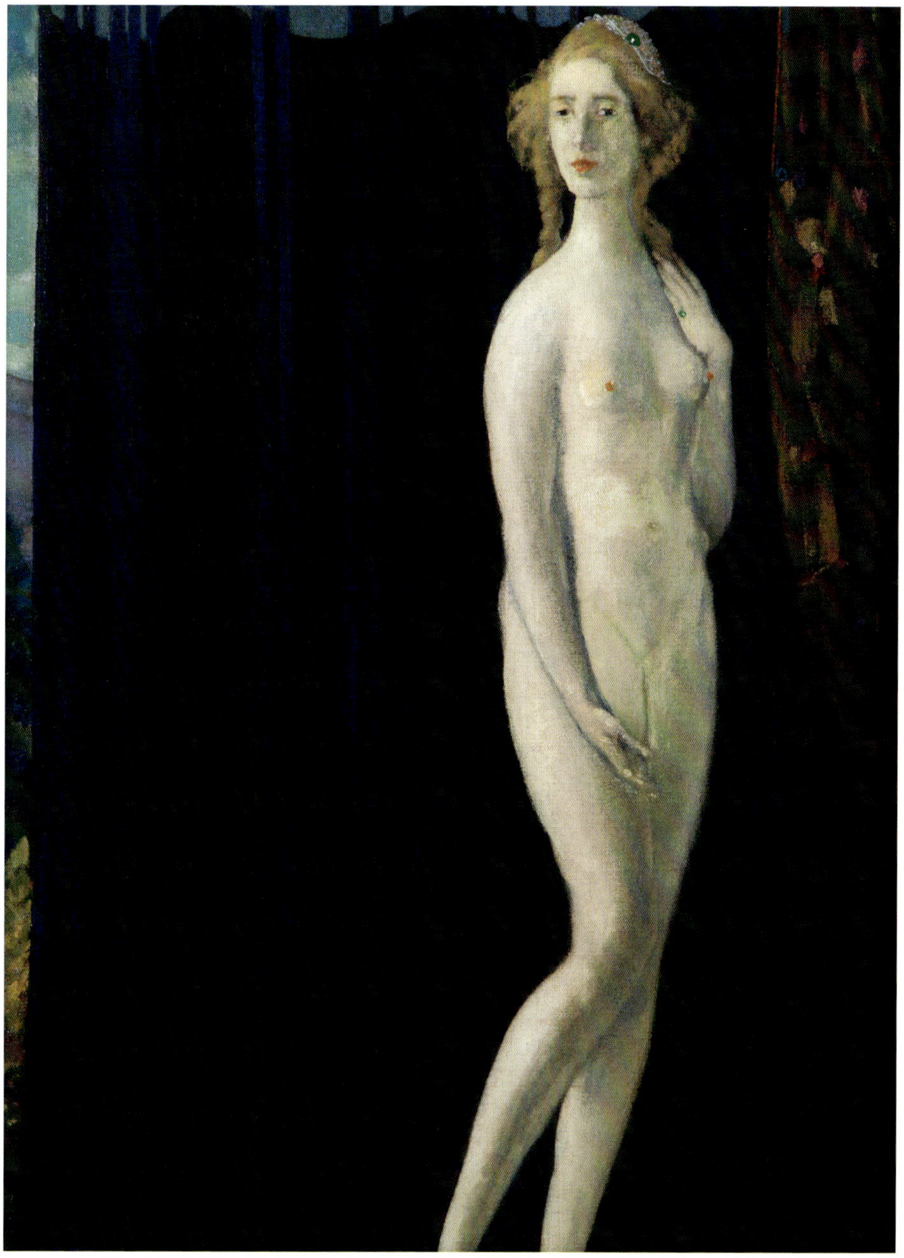

16. *Helen, the Dawn Flower*, c. 1908
Oil on canvas
Owen Yost Collection, Florida

ROBERT DAVIS / MICHAEL LANGLOIS

Representation—hyperreal, fantastic, and often grotesque—has been the mark of Chicago art since the early twentieth century. By drawing on the real world even if it had to be embellished with fantasy or raw emotion, Chicago artists distinguished themselves from their New York counterparts. Yet abstraction has also long had a grasp on the city's artists.

The present installation, *Living the Dream*, by the collaborative duo Robert Davis and Michael Langlois, engages the annals of abstraction, creating a web of connections and resonances across time, space, and the strata of visual culture. Here Davis/Langlois drew on disparate sources—the history of European and American modern art, and the ideologies and graphic symbols of punk and hardcore music. The duo's painstakingly rendered paintings of simple geometric forms simultaneously evoke Kazimir Malevich's Suprematist works and punk-rock album covers. Davis/Langlois's paintings are inspired not only by the visual affinities between Malevich and punk iconography, but also by their common search for purity of form and emotion expressed through art. *Screen*, the designed object that divides the exhibition space, is based on the decoration of rock guitarist Eddie Van Halen's Stratocaster, underscoring the potential to locate abstraction in the visual detritus of the everyday. By mining such a diverse array of sources, Davis/Langlois demonstrates the resurgent vitality of abstraction in Chicago art.

JAMES YOOD
(TEXT BY GREGORY J. HARRIS WITH DAVIS/LANGLOIS)

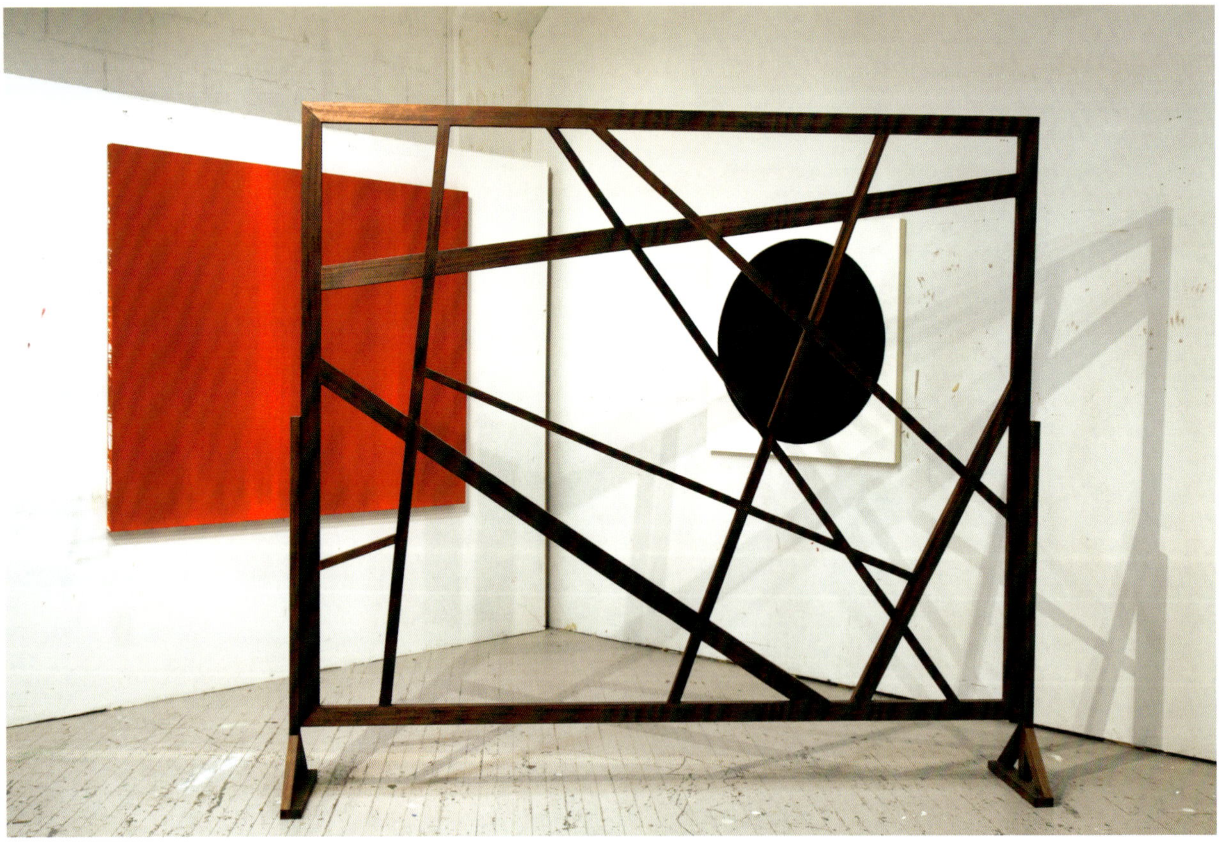

17. *Living the Dream*, 2011
Site-specific mixed-media installation
Collection of the artists; courtesy of moniquemeloche gallery, Chicago

MANIERRE DAWSON

During his lifetime, Manierre Dawson's art was virtually unknown, his role in the genesis of the American avant-garde not yet recognized. All that began to change in the late 1960s and early 1970s, when the first exhibitions and publications devoted to his work started to appear.

Dawson, who came from Chicago, earned a degree in civil engineering at his parents' urging, although he longed to study painting at the School of the Art Institute of Chicago. He subsequently worked at the architectural firm of Holabird & Roche. But his heart was in painting, and he spent his lunch hours in the Art Institute's galleries or library.

In 1910 Dawson took a sabbatical, ostensibly to view great monuments, but really to visit European museums. Either shortly before leaving on his journey or soon afterward, he executed a series of abstractions, culminating in the triptych *Prognostic*. *Differential Complex* was probably a study for the triptych, whose color scheme and forms it resembles. Certain Dawson scholars assert that these abstractions preceded those of Arthur Dove and Vassily Kandinsky. In the absence of any proof, it might be more accurate to state that all three artists were simultaneously searching for a new style for the new century.

Perhaps preoccupied with making art, Dawson lost his job and could not find steady work. In 1914 economic necessity forced a move to Michigan, where he became an orchard keeper. Farming and family life gradually absorbed his time, and he quit making art around 1920.

MARY GEDO

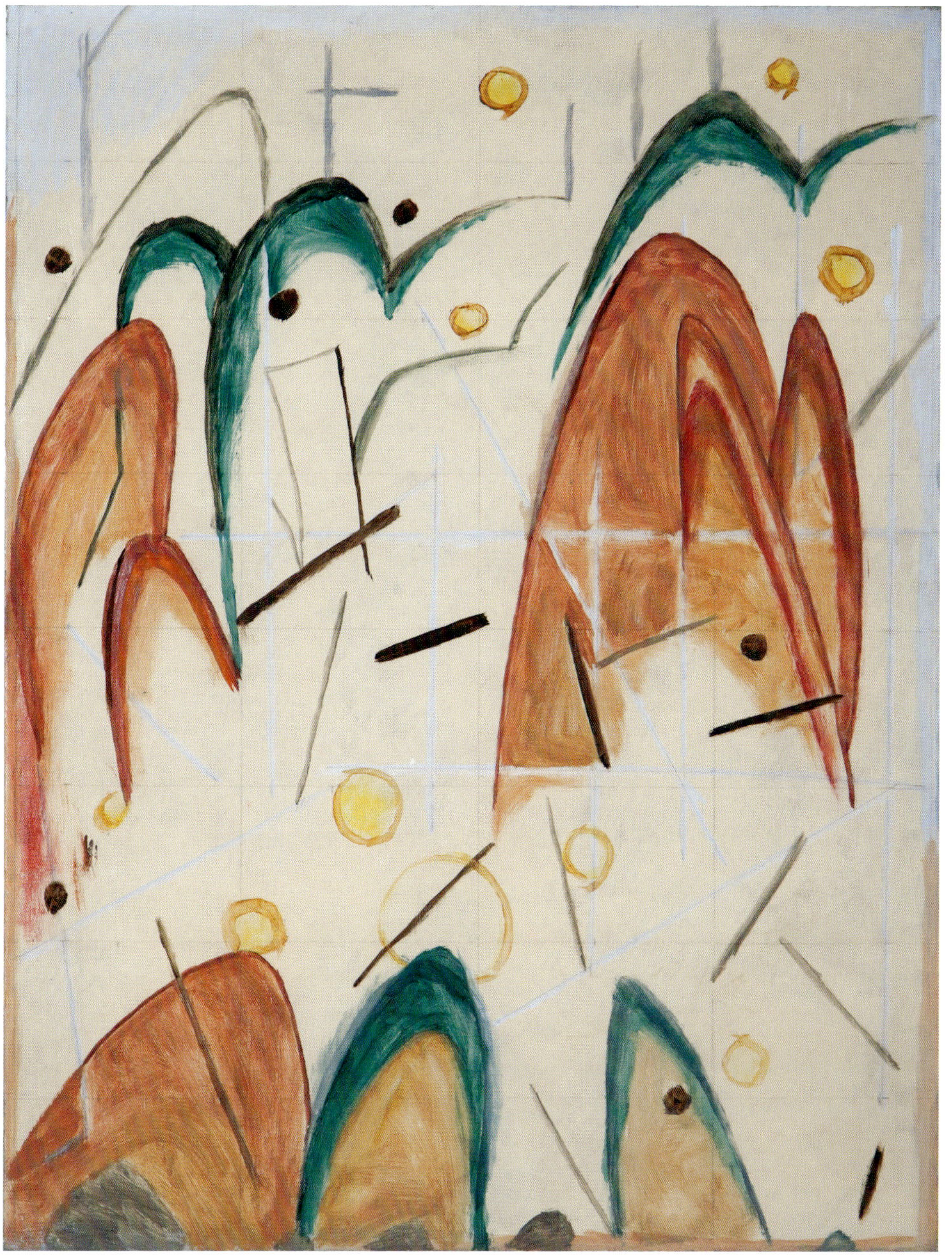

18. *Study for Differential Complex*, 1910 (?)
Oil on canvas
Collection of David and Mary Winton Green, Wilmette, Illinois

TONY FITZPATRICK

Tony Fitzpatrick has established himself as an important presence in Chicago's artistic landscape, not only as a writer, actor, and visual artist, but also as a staunch advocate for emerging and unrecognized artists. His new gallery, Firecat (formerly Big Cat Press Studio, where he worked as an artist for over seventeen years), has become a venue for aspiring artists from Chicago and elsewhere.

Fitzpatrick has long been a champion of the underdog, the overlooked, the shunned—whether the fallen baseball hero in *Our Joe*, a print from his *Remembered City* series, or the downtrodden hobos of the Great Depression that he depicted in his recent play, book, and collages entitled *This Train*. Even the common moth is deemed exceptional in Fitzpatrick's work. Describing his recent collage drawing *The Winter Tiger*, the artist noted, "I returned to making moths because they still speak to me in a way that sends ice through my veins, and yet I am awed by their beauty and otherness; their appetite for destruction and gorgeous flight. . . . Look up at any street lamp and you see them, slugging it out with the light, trying not to die." Fitzpatrick's empathetic and sometimes fierce storytelling makes him a visionary poet, artist, and performer, giving voice and humanity to the nameless.

LAURA FATEMI

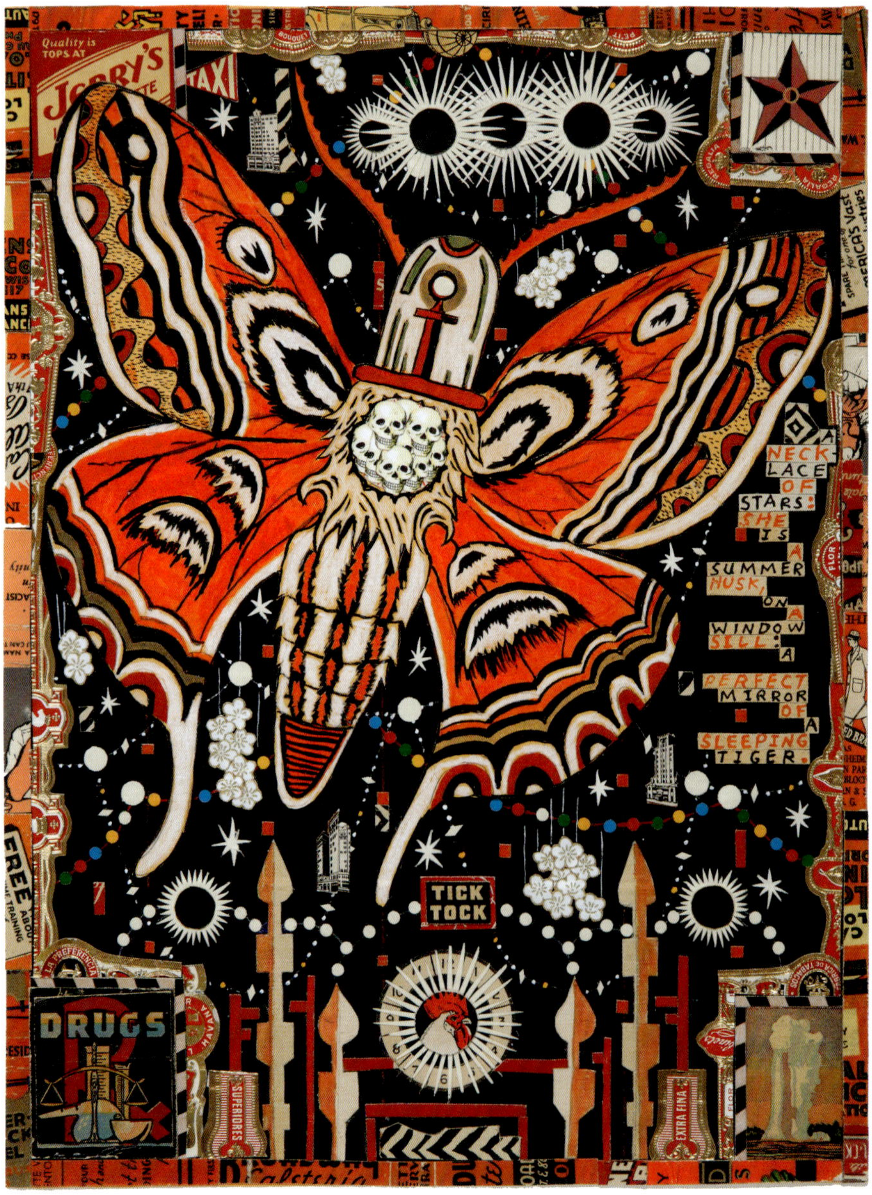

19. *The Winter Tiger*, 2010
Graphite, ink, pigment, and found materials on archival board
Collection of the DePaul Art Museum, Art Acquisition Endowment, 2010.70

RAMON GABRIEL

I am intrigued by the small watercolor painting *String Quartet* by Ramon Gabriel. It is filled with energy, and when you look at it you hear music—I think it has to be jazz! The players are bouncing off each other, and it looks like the space itself is moving. The artist could have chosen strong color, but the muted tones work in counterpoint to the vibrancy of the image and let him literally fill the air with sound.

Gabriel is not well known, but he was associated with the South Side Community Art Center, which was an important laboratory in Chicago for artistic collaboration—an environment like the Bauhaus. Segregation had turned the African American community inward, and people in different circles connected easily as a result. Artists, writers, and musicians documented many aspects of life: families, education, business, social and cultural events, community activism, and nightlife. The South Side Community Art Center was an important part of the community, and it helped artists to be more prolific, connected, and quick to share ideas and knowledge. It is not surprising that Gabriel would choose a musical subject, and find a way to show it that integrates sound and image so beautifully.

CAROL ADAMS

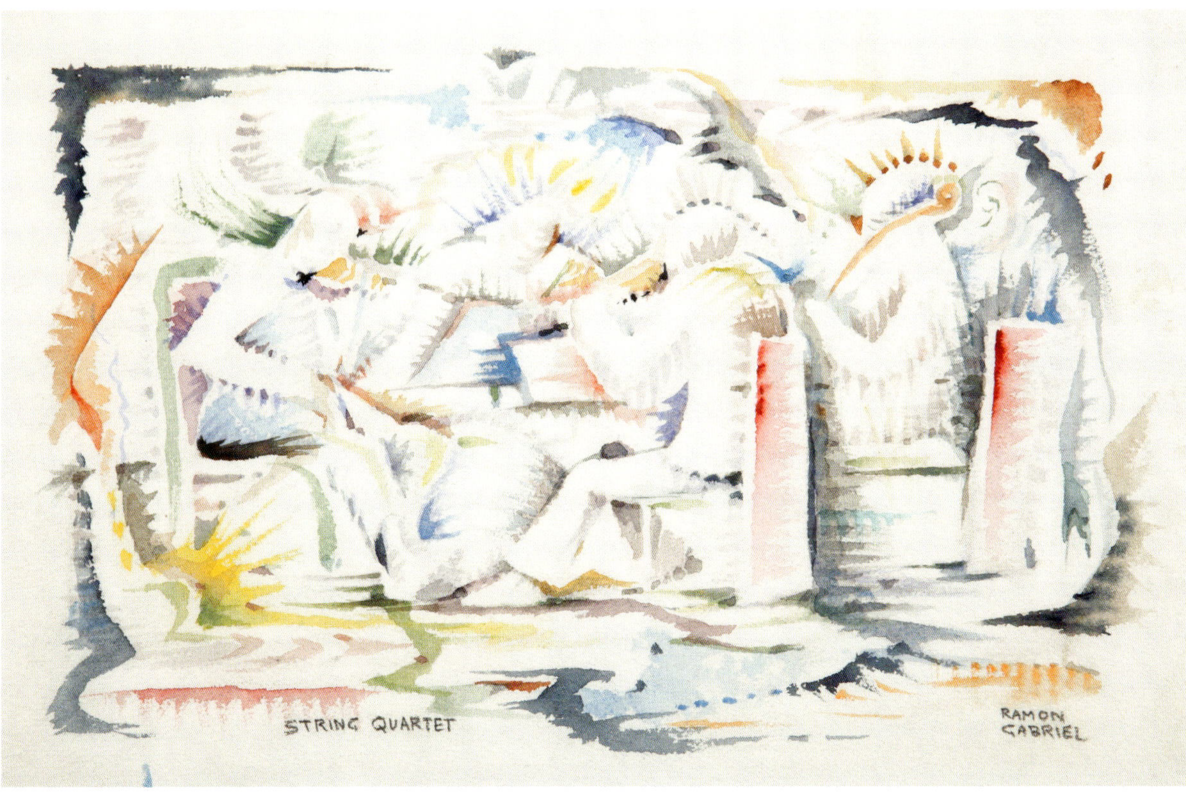

20. *String Quartet*, c. 1945
Watercolor on paper
Collection of the DePaul Museum of Art,
Art Acquisition Endowment, 2010.4

GEORGE HEALY

The need for further examination of the history of Chicago art is evident from the example of George Healy. Visitors to the Newberry Library may have seen some of Healy's portraits, but the city's art world as a whole lacks any substantial knowledge of his luminous career as a portraitist. Consider the following: in 1913 the Art Institute of Chicago mounted a centennial exhibition of Healy's work, undertaken in recognition of his striking accomplishments as a portraitist to the wealthy and famous.

Even now his range of subjects alone is impressive. Among the Americans who sat for Healy were presidents John Quincy Adams, Ulysses Grant, Abraham Lincoln, and John Tyler; statesmen John Calhoun, Henry Clay, and Daniel Webster; and foreigners of consequence Chancellor Otto von Bismarck of Germany, Hungarian composer Franz Liszt, and King Louis-Philippe of France. His work was in such demand in Europe that he crossed the Atlantic more than thirty times. Stylistically, Healy was a straightforward realist with a command of the medium that can be measured by the importance of the people he portrayed. Regrettably, we do not know the identity of the subject in this work.

With all due respect to the Chicago artists who are well remembered by history, not one of them has a catalogue of subjects as renowned as Healy's. It is past time for Chicago's art community to elevate Healy to the level of the city's creative elite.

FRANZ SCHULZE

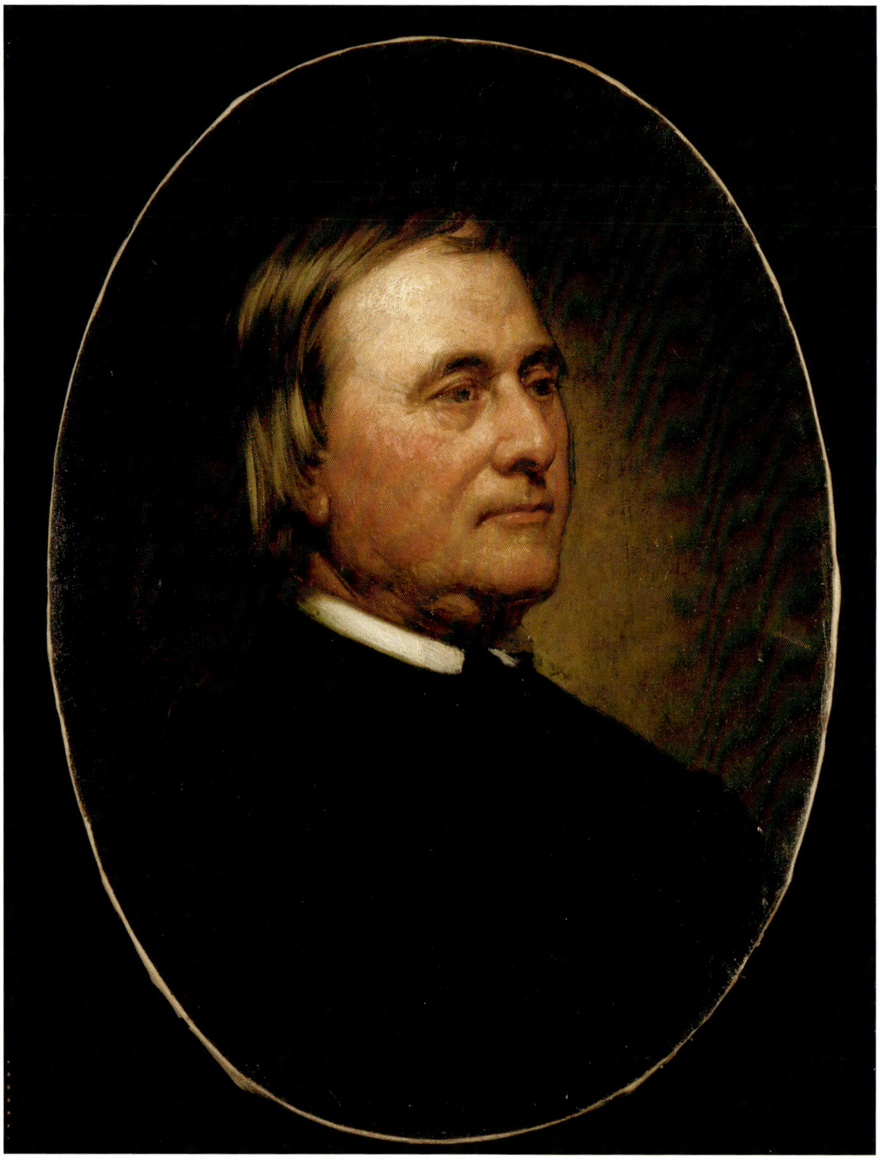

21. *Portrait Bust of a Man*, 1865
Oil on canvas
Collection of the Terra Foundation for American Art,
gift of Mr. and Mrs. John Estabrook, C1983.5

CARL HOECKNER

A young prodigy, primed by generations of German craftsmen. A refugee, welcomed by Chicago's professional artists. Suddenly, angrily transformed by World War I. And thereafter dedicated to what he called the "bitter truth."

Other artists celebrated Chicago's picturesque neighborhoods, its gleaming bridges, its inventive skyscrapers. But Carl Hoeckner painted bemedaled Mussolinis reigning over striptease dancers and hypnotized crowds. Other Chicago artists sent their work to established exhibitions, but Hoeckner and his friends invented radical groups: the Chicago No-Jury Society, the Cor-Ardens, the Independents. He *tried* to explain the Armory Show when it came to Chicago. He *tried* to transform the Art Institute's jury system. But what persisted, he said, was the "bitter truth."

In *Cold Steel*, the workers have become machines. Jaws clenched, eyes narrowed, muscles tense, they defy any threat. The soldiers below, helmeted and armed with machine guns, add "the military" to "the industrial" equation. Although each face is different, every arm, every wheel, every instrument growls their unity.

Hoeckner's was a varied career: elegant commercial designer, Federal Arts Project studio leader, School of the Art Institute of Chicago professor, political missionary. Although most of Hoeckner's paintings were destroyed, his graphics are in many important public and private collections.

ESTHER SPARKS

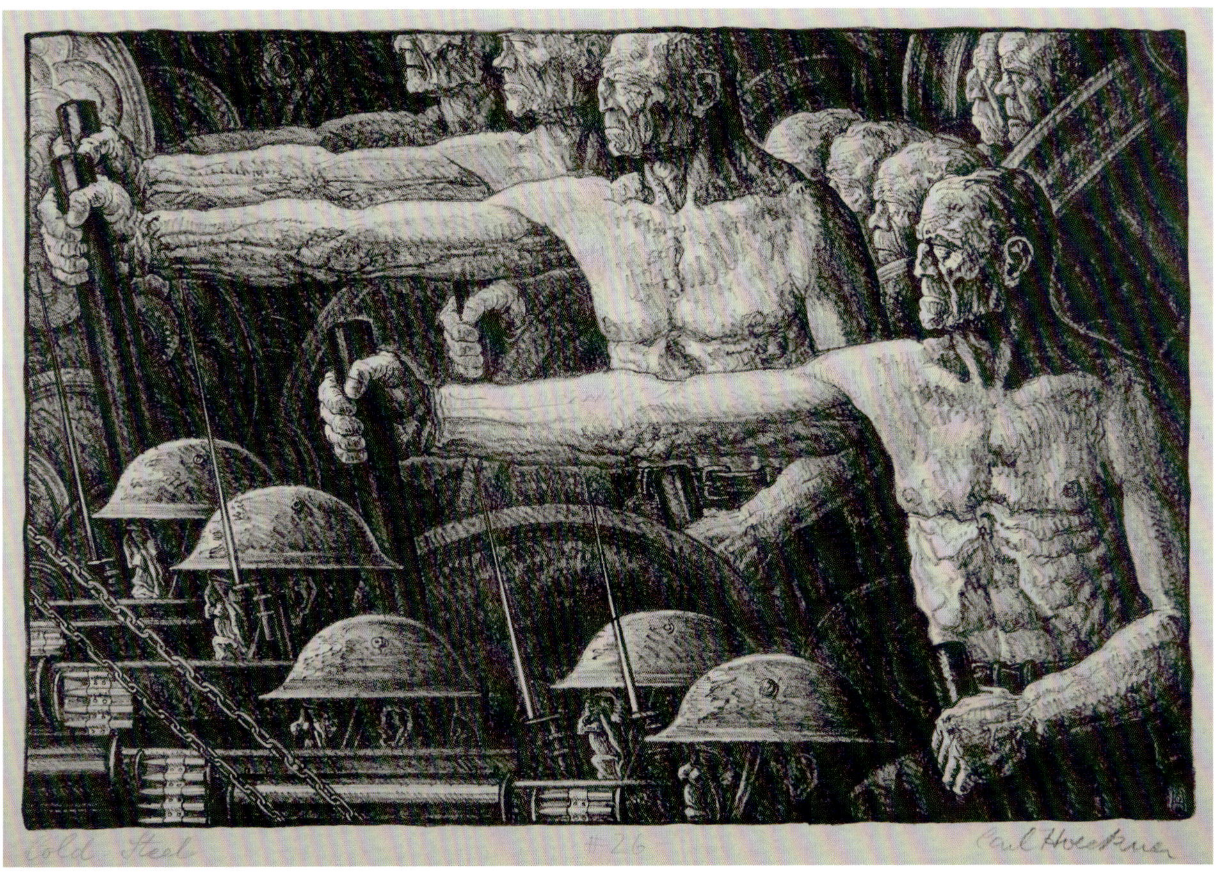

22. *Cold Steel*, c. 1935
Lithograph on paper
Mary and Leigh Block Museum of Art,
Northwestern University, 1995.50.24

SHANE HUFFMAN

Shane Huffman makes powerfully original works of art that fuse a passion for esoteric aspects of science with highly personal explorations of human behavior. Early on these interests were centered on astronomy and performative actions that were invested with symbolic significance. "Finished" works by Huffman were often configured in apparently informal but carefully studied installations that combined photography, drawings, objects, quotations, and more. Huffman willfully blended and confused science and art, fact and fiction, self and alter ego. Many of those early environments evoked a scientist's lab or the workshop of a fictitious investigator or researcher.

Huffman's work with photography, in particular, continues to be investigative and experimental. In 2009 he subjected silver gelatin on photographic paper to microwave rays. Evidence of this irradiation emerged in the form of cosmic color patterns reminiscent of psychedelic Rorschach inkblots. This print was made by melting silver—the silver chloride ($AgCl$) and silver bromide ($AgBr$) contained in photographic paper begin to melt at 852 degrees Fahrenheit. The artist used a heat gun to blast the sheet with temperatures as high as 1,000 degrees Fahrenheit, releasing pure silver onto the charred surface of the photograph. The resulting image resembles a crude model of a lunar landscape. Huffman's unique brand of rudimentary, homemade alchemy generates images that are oddly tough, strangely beautiful, and surprisingly compelling.

JAMES RONDEAU

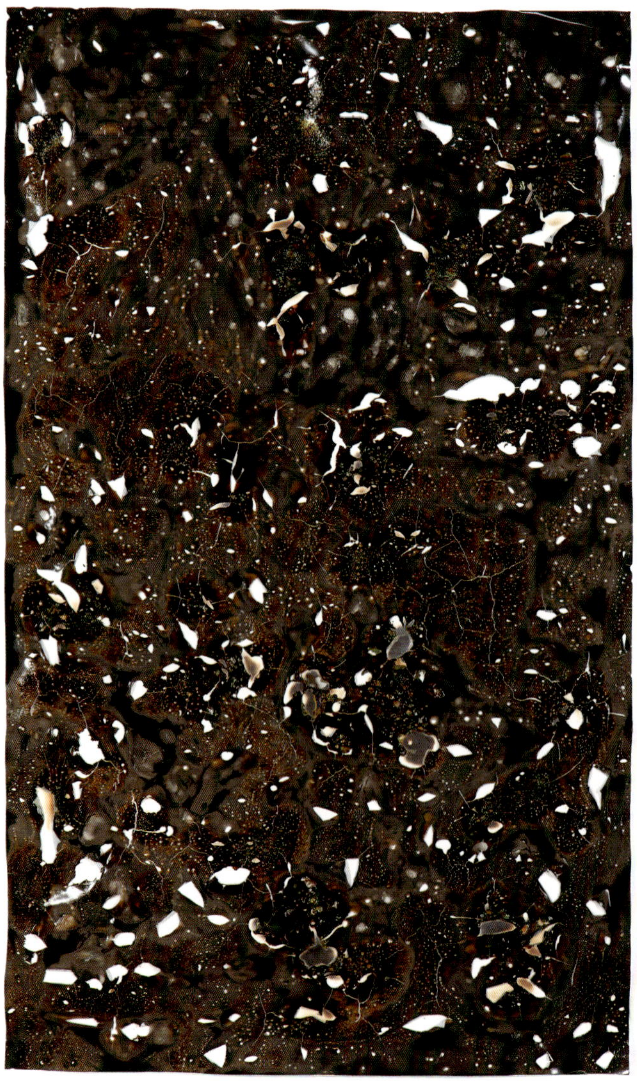

23. *I'm Not an Alchemist, but I Do Work in Metals*, 2011
Gelatin silver print
Collection of the DePaul Art Museum, Art Acquisition Endowment, 2011.10

RICHARD HUNT

Flight Forms is a stunning sculpture and Chicago landmark located at 59th Street and Cicero Avenue, at the edge of Midway Airport, which it honors with sweeping majesty. It is one of Richard Hunt's most evocative works, suggesting several perspectives on the wonder of flight and the unbridled freedom that is so much a part of soaring through the skies. The piece is experiential: with grace and dignity, the artist reminded us that flight is a profound challenge to the law of gravity—and that soaring upward off the ground has aesthetic dimension as well.

My husband and I were both friends and great admirers of Hunt long before we acquired his work. A few years ago, on our thirty-fifth wedding anniversary, my husband surprised me with the gift of the maquette of *Flight Forms*. It remains a very special part of our home, which is not far from the thirty-five-foot sculpture's position at the airport. Since then we have gotten to know Hunt in a whole new way. We have acquired several pieces of his sculpture that bring a sense of drama and refinement to our home. Living with these works has deepened our friendship with the artist and has helped to recalibrate our perceptions and expectations, as all great art should.

ANNE AND ED BURKE

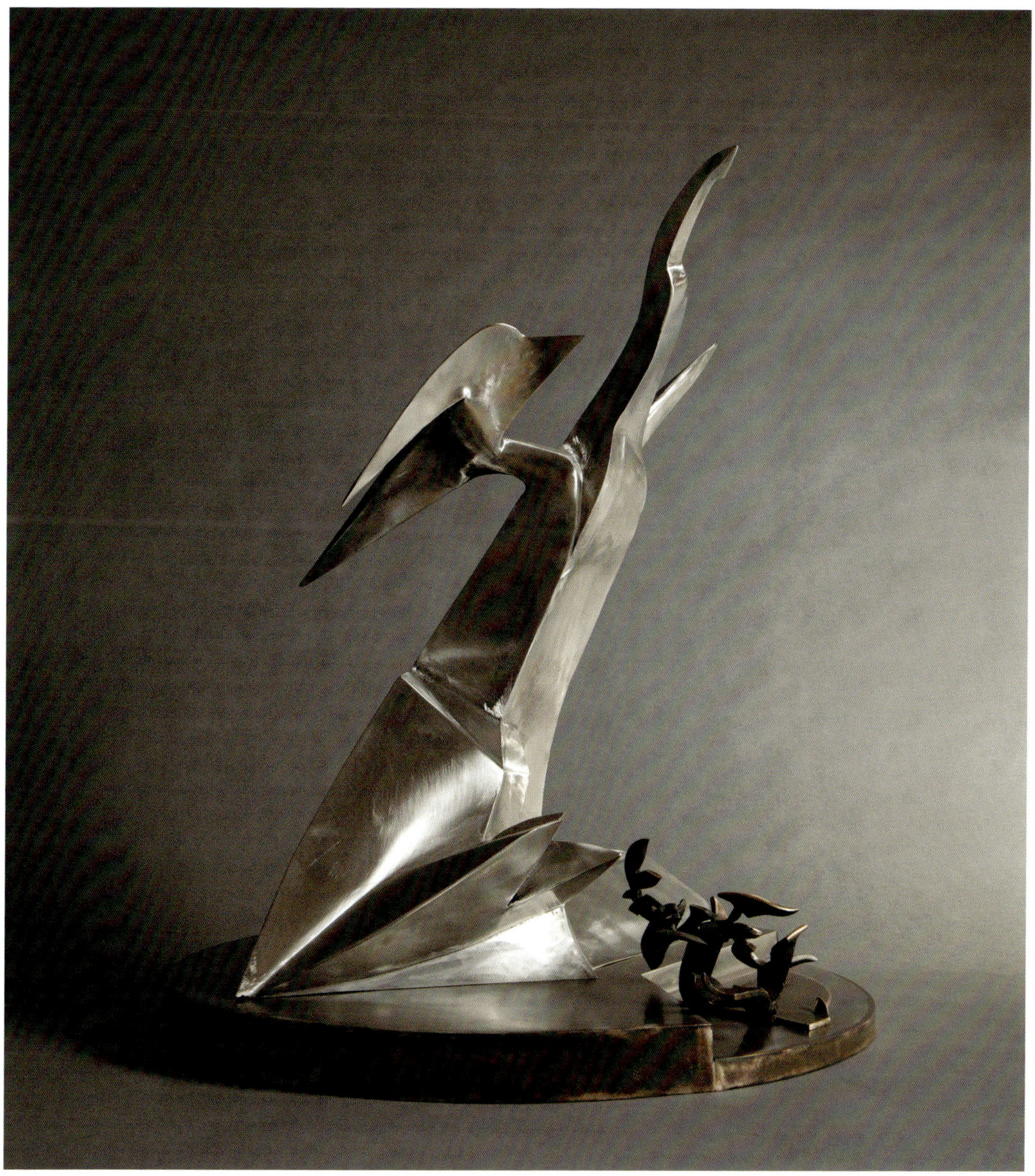

24. *Flight Forms*, 2002
Steel
Collection of Anne and Ed Burke

MARGARET IANNELLI

Had Margaret Iannelli aspired to become a famous artist in the usual sense of the term, she would have found an incredible number of obstacles in her path. It was challenging for female artists to gain critical recognition in early-twentieth-century Chicago, and she chose to work with relative anonymity in the seldom-appreciated artistic field of commercial illustration and graphic design. Her own presence was overshadowed by that of her flamboyant artist-husband, Alfonso Iannelli, and many of the best works she created under the auspices of their collaborative Iannelli Studios came to be erroneously attributed to him alone. Another challenge was that mental illness necessitated institutional care for over half her life. But even under these adverse circumstances, she continued to create remarkably strong work. Ultimately Margaret Iannelli achieved success on her own terms. The creative atmosphere of Iannelli Studios was driven by contemporary democratic ideals for art and society, including personal contact with such figures as architect Frank Lloyd Wright and political revolutionary Emma Goldman. For Margaret Iannelli, success was not about recognition in the rarefied world of galleries and museums; rather, she quietly placed vibrant modern art in people's everyday lives through the media of advertising, illustration, and commercial design. She was particularly interested in giving children comfortable encounters with contemporary design, such as this 1916 cover for an unpublished adaptation of a Hans Christian Andersen story.

TIM SAMUELSON

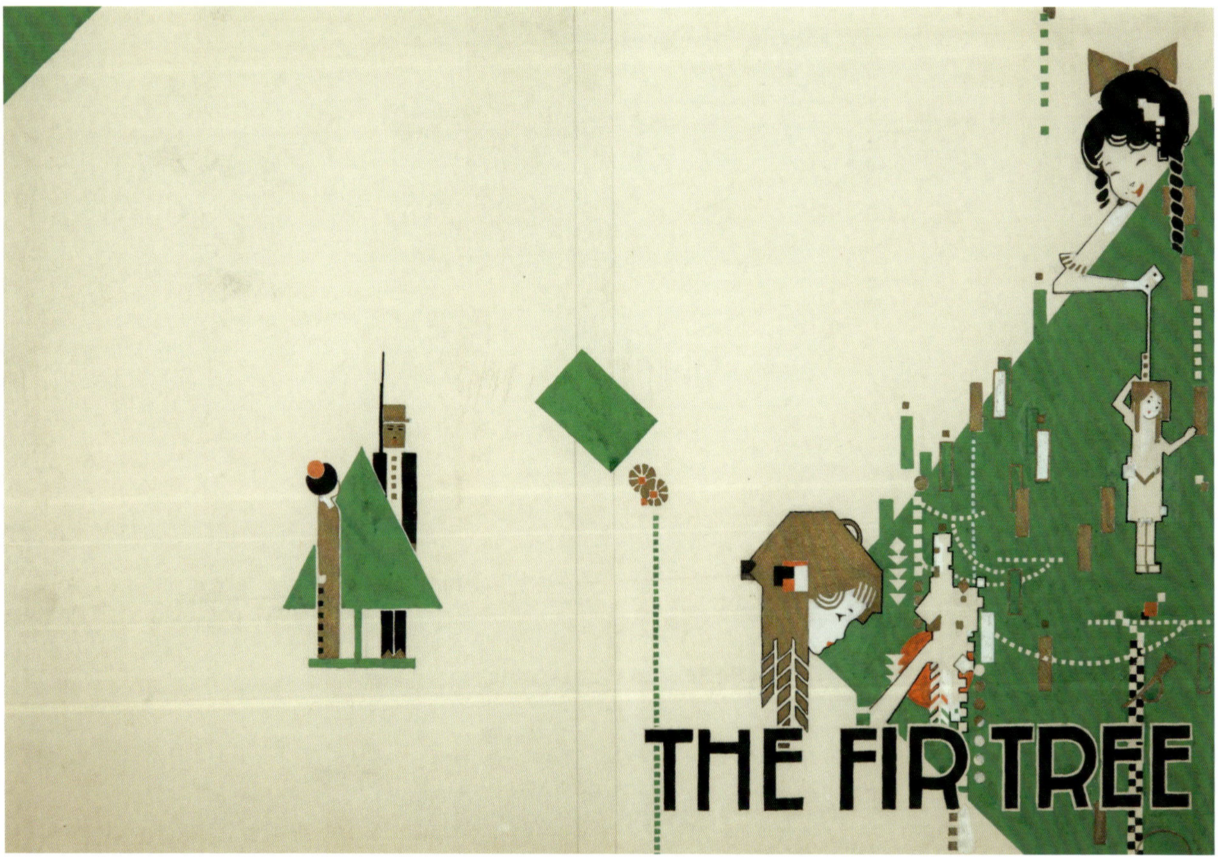

25. Cover design for *The Fir Tree*, 1916
Ink and graphite on paper
Collection of Tim Samuelson

A. RAYMOND KATZ

A. Raymond Katz, who also used the name Sandor, is not unknown, but I would say that he probably is obscure. A Hungarian immigrant who came to Chicago (after New York) by the early 1920s, he was simultaneously a commercial artist, a painter, a muralist (for the Century of Progress World's Fair), a gallery owner, a poster maker for the theater corporation Balaban and Katz, and, in later years, a creator of synagogue art. He was also the most prolific producer of covers for *The Chicagoan*, a short-lived but urbane local magazine of the 1920s. With his ethnic roots, commercial ties, extraordinary versatility, commitment to contemporary art, interest in depicting Chicago scenes, and, above all, creative imagination, he deserves to be better known.

The Argument presents a quintessential confrontation, perhaps in the friendly confines of Wrigley Field. The ball players seem locked into theatrical poses, almost as if waiting for a studio photographer to record the scene. The hot-dog vendor, on the other hand, is intent on making his sale, which, to judge from the coin being proffered, is at an appropriate Depression-era price.

NEIL HARRIS

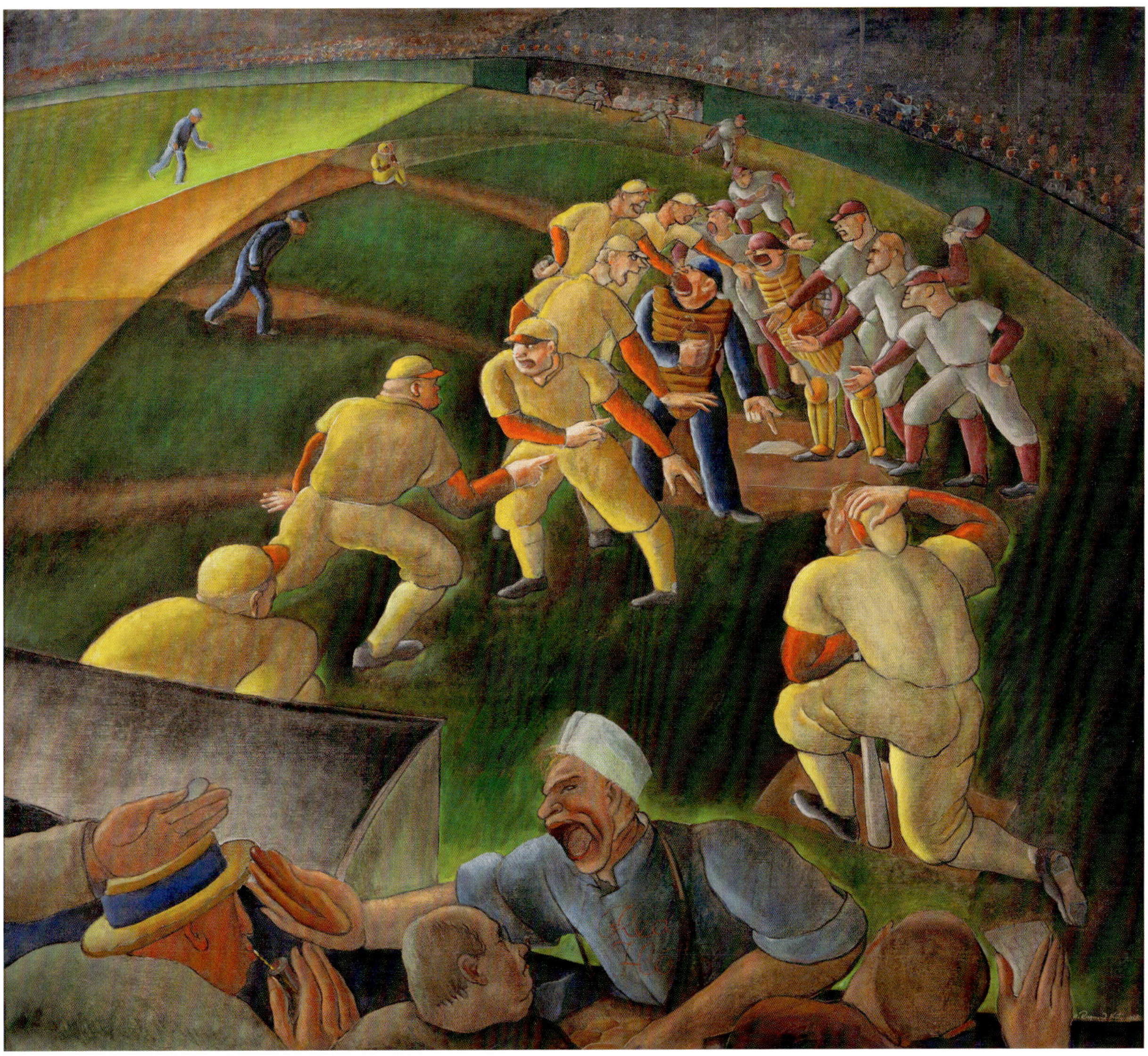

26. *The Argument*, 1938
Oil on canvas
Collection of Barry and Merle Gross

WESLEY KIMLER

Wesley Kimler is one of the best painters of our time. Fluent in myriad styles—from abstraction to realism—he can put onto canvas any image or form he wants. He is a painter's painter and eschews much of what is going on in the world's art centers. He does not work to satisfy an audience; instead, he works to overwhelm it with the content, stature, and power of his imagery. His paintings are often huge—sometimes as large as ten by thirty feet. They are heroic statements about brave, obdurate, or inspirational human endeavor, addressing issues of life, death, and the pursuit of excellence.

Kimler takes control of his art, his output, and his career. He does not suffer fools or the nonsensical aspects of the art world—sometimes to his own detriment. For him, quality is more important than convenience, integrity more significant than contrivance, and honest technique a prerequisite for being considered an artist at all. It is rare to find someone who embraces technology, reads prolifically, knows precisely what is going on in remote portions of the globe, and maintains a strict allegiance to what has become old-school—a painter who paints and insists that good technique is mandatory. Kimler is that person.

PAUL KLEIN

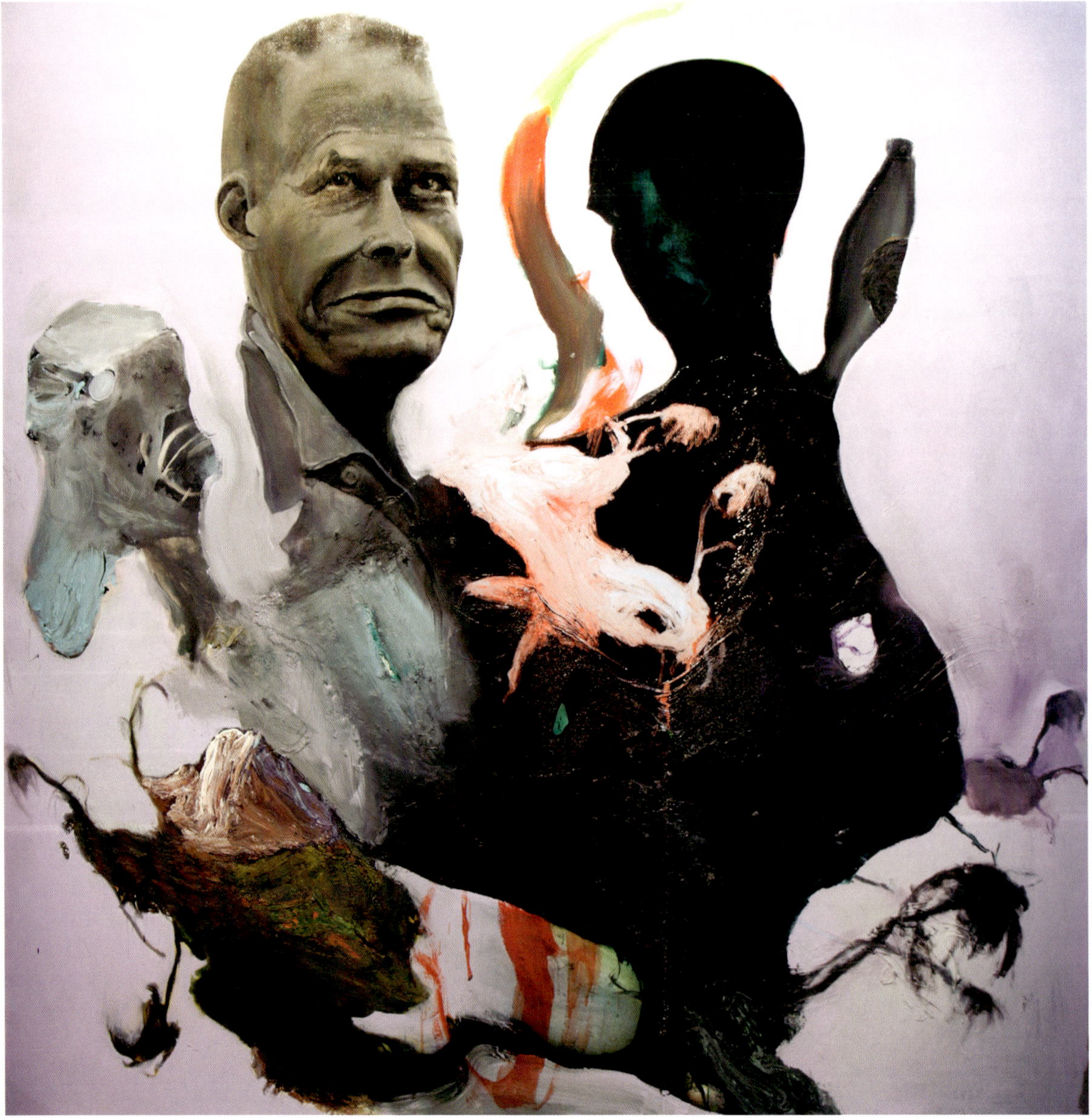

27. *Five Sisters*, 2010
Oil on canvas
Collection of the artist

ELLEN LANYON

Ellen Lanyon's private mythology encompasses several dual realities: fear and delight, right and wrong, interior and exterior. Each of her paintings represents a moment of time, a piece of a visual—even theatrical—narrative in which land, water, animals, and her collected objects coexist. And each manifests her interest in environmental issues, science, magic, and humor. *The Italian Box* lives in these dual realities as an interior object located in an idyllic exterior space. The snake (a symbol of life to some and danger to many) enters the box by its own means, perhaps serving as the reluctant or tardy guardian of the forbidden candies carefully placed outside it. The snake's choice to curl up in the interior tempts us to consider grabbing a piece of chocolate, since it appears the snake is just far enough away for us to do so. Or have we been magically tricked to fall for this illusion of safety?

Lanyon's artistic practice formed during the uncertain decade of the 1960s, while she was living in Chicago. The time and place informed her artistic practice and fostered her independence as an art maker and thinker. She continues to be an active and respected artist today, and her quiet influence hovers over many in this city, myself included.

MARY ANN PAPANEK-MILLER

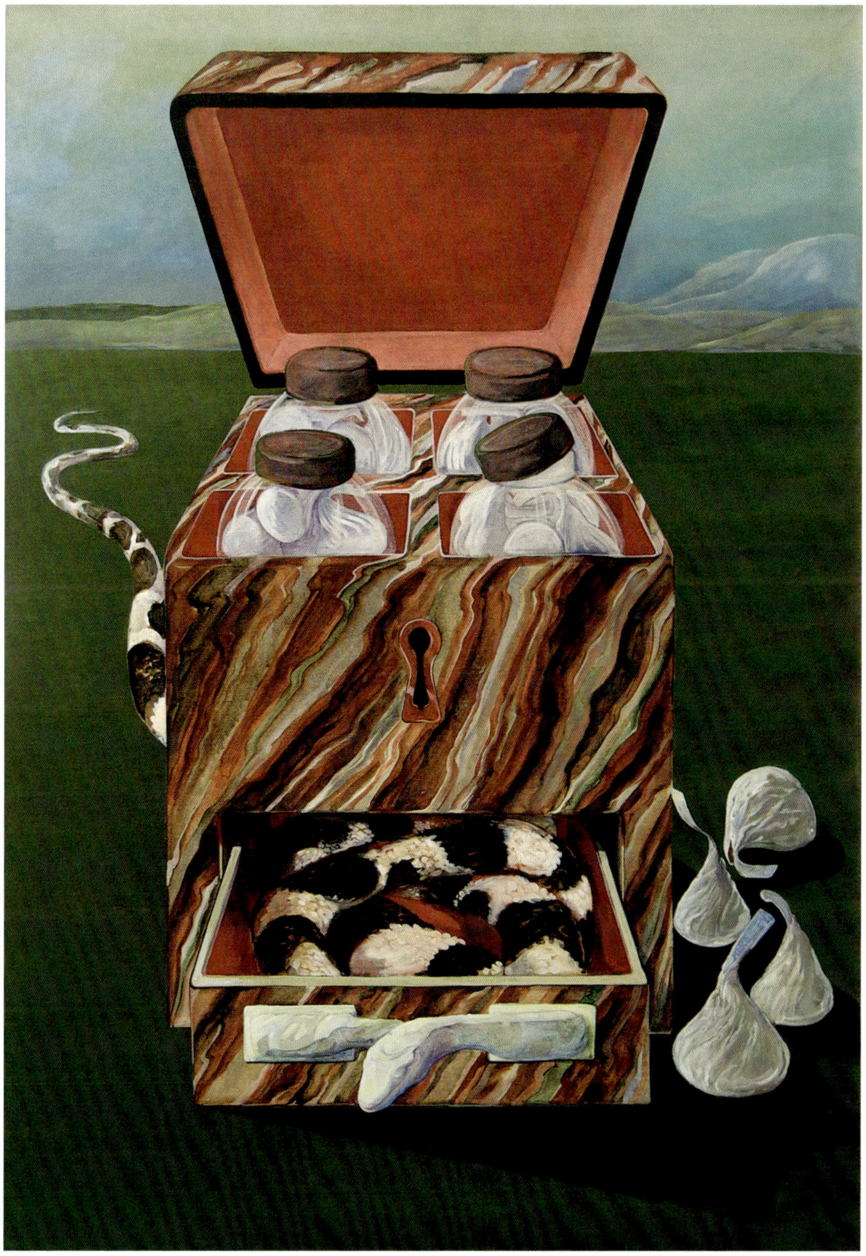

28. *The Italian Box*, 1973
Oil on canvas
Collection of the artist;
courtesy of Valerie Carberry Gallery

KERRY JAMES MARSHALL

I have known and admired Kerry James Marshall's work for more than twenty years. I saw this painting when I made a visit to his studio, and I chose it because I was intrigued by the figure of the artist. He is in shadow, and every time I look at the image I have to adjust my eye to see him. It is about seeing and at the same time not seeing.

I am also interested in Marshall's use of color. Here it is predominantly a black of a very rich and varied tonality and a lot of pink, which seems unexpected, though these are the colors the artist uses most often. The black is a stunning, beautiful color. I am not sure what the pink area represents—another painting? a textile? In one part of the pink area, the picture seems as if it is unfinished, and there are faint numbers visible. The more you look, the more you see.

LEWIS MANILOW

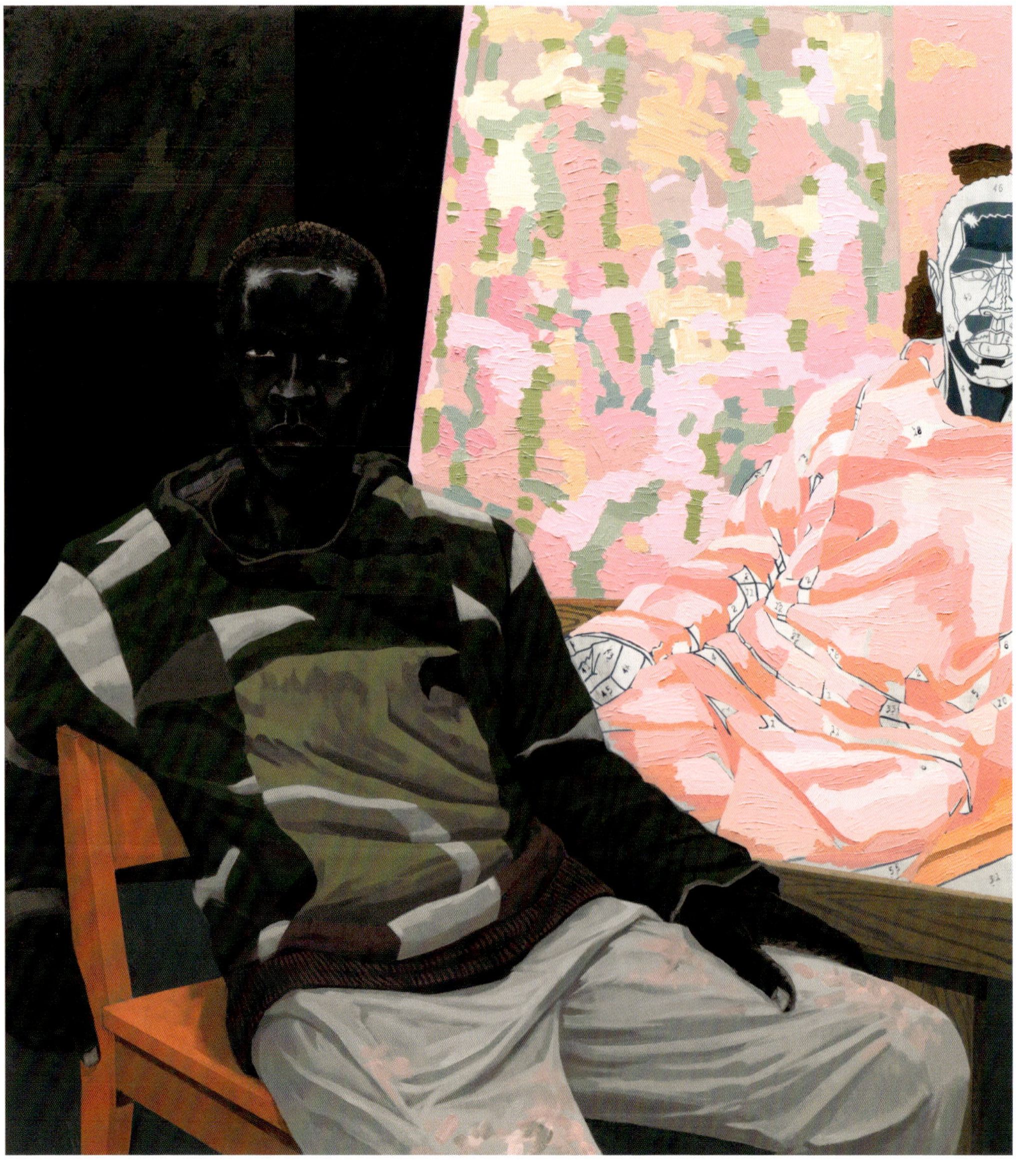

29. *Untitled (Painter)*, 2010
Acrylic on PVC panel
Collection of Lewis Manilow, Chicago

ARCHIBALD MOTLEY

Although we have about fifty Chicago artists represented in our collection of ninety-two paintings, Archibald Motley was the one whose work I had most wanted to own since I began to focus on Chicago art exclusively. Motley was the first African American to graduate from the School of the Art Institute of Chicago, and his abundant talent is evident in this portrait, which is unusual both in the sitter's downcast gaze and in the fact that, unlike most of his subjects, she does not appear to be African American. *Knitting Girl* had been taken off its stretcher and rolled when Barbara and I first saw it in 2007. Even though it showed some surface dirt, the painting had great charm and appeal, which cleaning only enhanced. We were very pleased to acquire it as the final addition to our collection.

POWELL BRIDGES

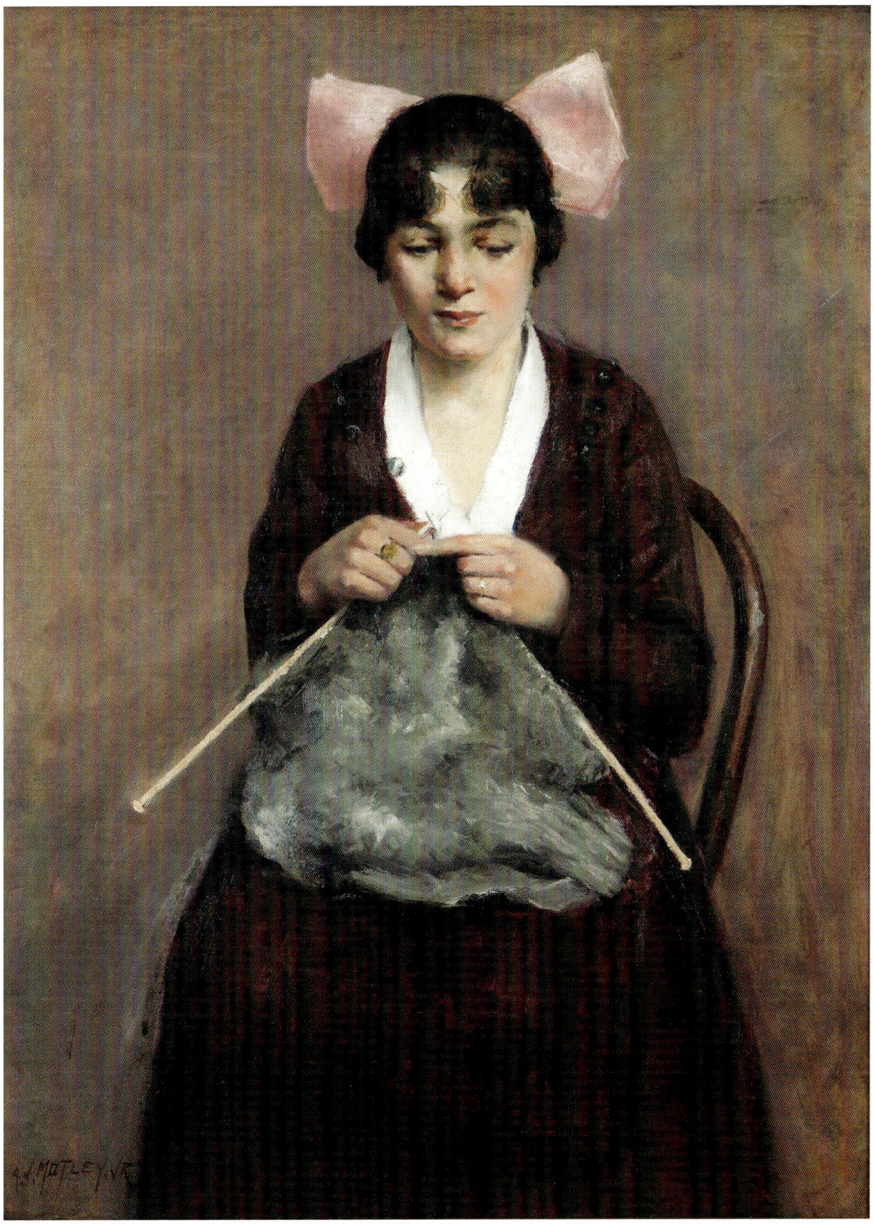

30. *Knitting Girl*, c. 1920
Oil on canvas
Bridges Collection, Powell and Barbara Bridges

GREGORY ORLOFF

Gregory Orloff was an extraordinarily versatile Chicago artist: a photographer, creative experimental printmaker, draftsman, and book illustrator, producing everything from children's books to scathing pen-and-ink cartoons depicting Presidents Johnson and Nixon during the Vietnam era. After he and his wife died, almost 1,000 prints and drawings were found in their house. His greater achievements, his paintings, were discovered in a chicken coop behind the house. Among these are *Spring Song*, shown at the Art Institute of Chicago in 1930, and *Paris Pavilion*, which was done during the 1933 Century of Progress World's Fair. These two paintings are remarkable because of the comingling of different races as equals. In *Spring Song*, three children sit on the front steps of a home singing together. Two are black and one is white. In *Paris Pavilion*, a white woman is seated at a table with a black man. The nearly nude dancer in front of their table (who also appears in a number of Orloff's drawings) is black, while the dancers behind her on stage are white.

While the political satire of his Johnson and Nixon drawings is not unusual, Orloff's depiction of racial equality goes back to at least 1930 and sets him apart from all other Chicago artists. Of the hundreds of paintings by Chicagoans that I have seen from the 1920s and 1930s, I cannot remember a single other example in which blacks and whites are shown as equals.

HARLAN J. BERK

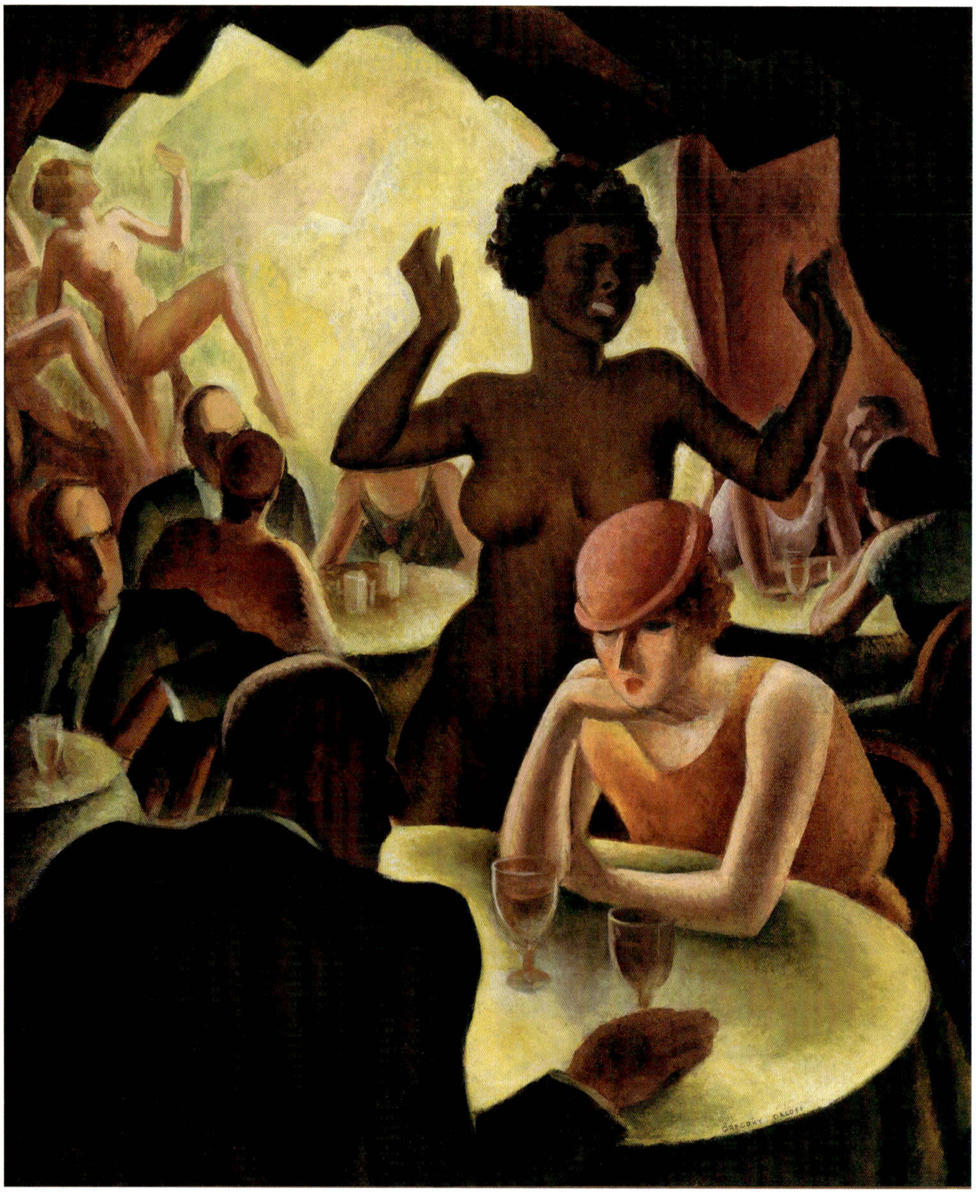

31. *Paris Pavilion*, 1933
Oil on canvas
Collection of Mr. and Mrs. Harlan J. Berk

ANGEL OTERO

Angel Otero's painting is informed by memories of his past and art-historical references to the Baroque, modernist painters such as Phillip Guston and Willem de Kooning, and more recent Neo-Expressionists like Georg Baselitz. Importantly, his works rely on his keen understanding of process, emphasizing the material qualities of his medium through the manipulation and build-up of paint on canvas. With these tools, Otero constructs works with successive layers of impasto paint, a process that shuttles the viewer's focus between two and three dimensions, past and present imagery, giving the paintings a temporal quality, in which time and space fluctuate back and forth between surface and image.

There is a sense of pathos in Otero's paintings, due both to his deeply personal subject matter and to his effort to retrieve for the present an image of that which has passed yet still possesses the vitality to inform current aesthetics. This is not nostalgia or longing for remembrances of things past. On the contrary, the expressionist force that has its periodic reappearance in the art of the twentieth, and now the twenty-first, century reminds us that art is made with a pulse. Otero's painting brings a freshness to the expressionist vocabulary that argues for the continuity of painting as a viable medium.

ED MALDONADO

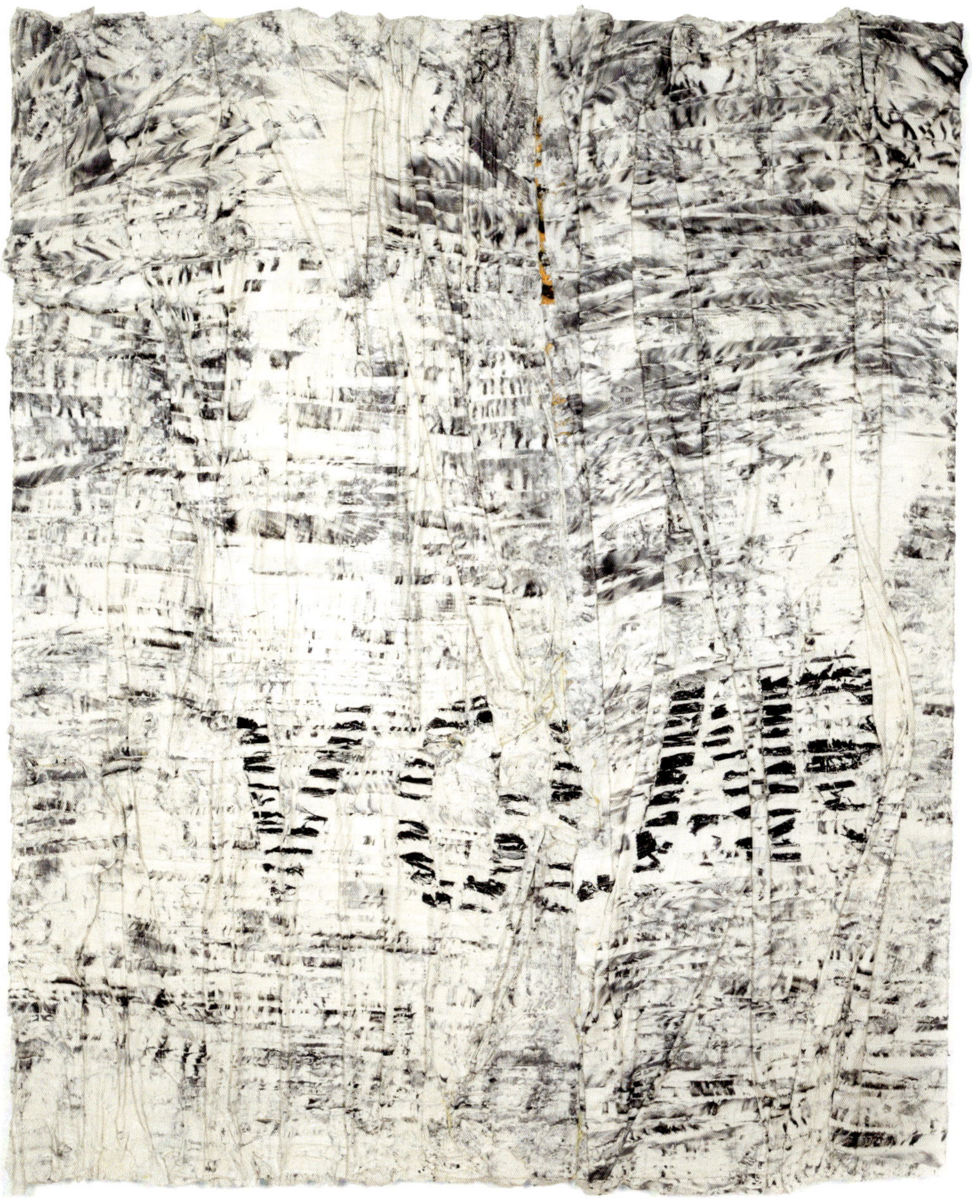

32. *Volar*, 2011
Collaged oil-paint skins on canvas
Collection of the DePaul Art Museum,
Art Acquisition Endowment, 2011.5

IRVING PETLIN

Irving Petlin, though cognizant of the formal achievements of abstract modernism, has persevered in expressing his imagination in a figurative mode. He was born in Chicago and studied at the School of the Art Institute of Chicago. Though he has lived in Paris, Los Angeles, and New York, Petlin's formative years in Chicago shaped his entire oeuvre. Early on he experimented with the dominant Abstract Expressionist style, but upon seeing the Post-Impressionist and Surrealist work that had such a presence in the artistic life of Chicago, he began his exploration of the unquiet human figure. European art on view across the city was a significant influence on Petlin's work.

Petlin was part of the generation of artists known as the Monster Roster, who came of age in the years following World War II. These artists were no longer satisfied with pure abstraction. For them a formalist approach seemed inadequate for the expression of postwar anxiety and anomie. This early painting marks Petlin's transition from abstraction to gestural figuration. It anticipates his mature work, which actively addresses social and political issues by mediating between figuration and abstraction in an expression of deep outrage and grief.

This text was adapted from "Irving Petlin: The Committed Brushstroke," by Peter Selz, published in the March 2010 issue of Art in America.

PETER SELZ

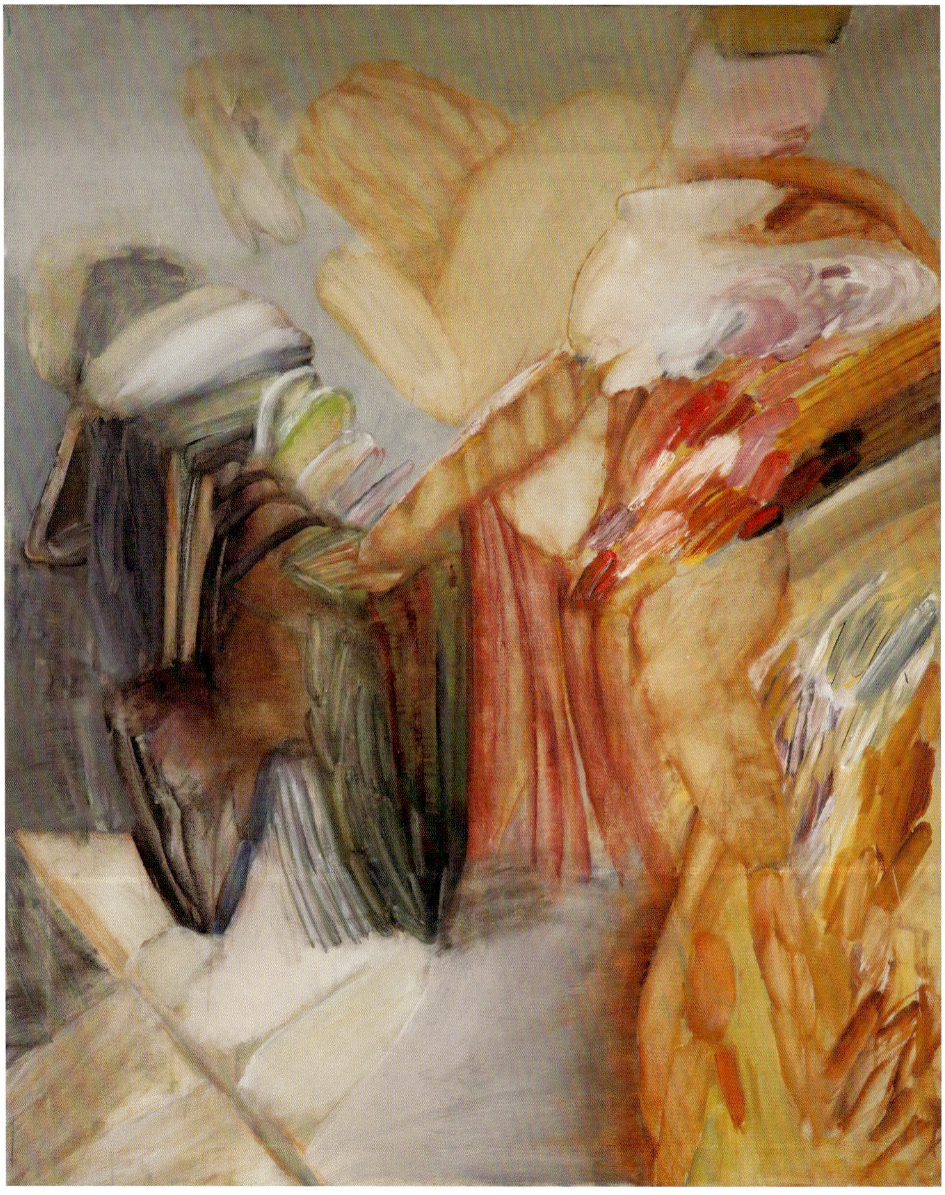

33. *Untitled*, 1955
Oil on canvas
Collection of the DePaul Art Museum,
Art Acquisition Endowment, 2011.9

CHRISTINA RAMBERG

Beginning in the 1960s, the painter Christina Ramberg depicted the female torso, typically truncated at the neck and knees and armored in tight-fitting girdles, lacy corsets, and "pointy-bust" bras. She often portrayed the backs of women's heads, delineating hair that curled and twisted into complicated knots. The face, however, was always absent. Plumbing fashion illustrations, etiquette manuals, lingerie catalogs, and medical illustrations from an earlier era while painting in the sober colors of ocher, brown, and black, Ramberg portrayed lingerie and hairstyles that evoke the 1940s and 1950s. And yet her imagery does not merely mimic her popular-culture sources. The extra darts, seams, and insets transform these undergarments into ornate, slightly threatening, and unusable apparel, while the hairstyles are impossibly complicated. Because of the ways in which Ramberg altered her sources, her works from the 1960s offered a proto-feminist critique of beauty culture in the days before the feminist art movement took hold in Chicago. Attractive and repulsive, poetic and political, Ramberg's imagery still speaks to us today about gender and the aesthetic distortion of the body.

CECILE WHITING

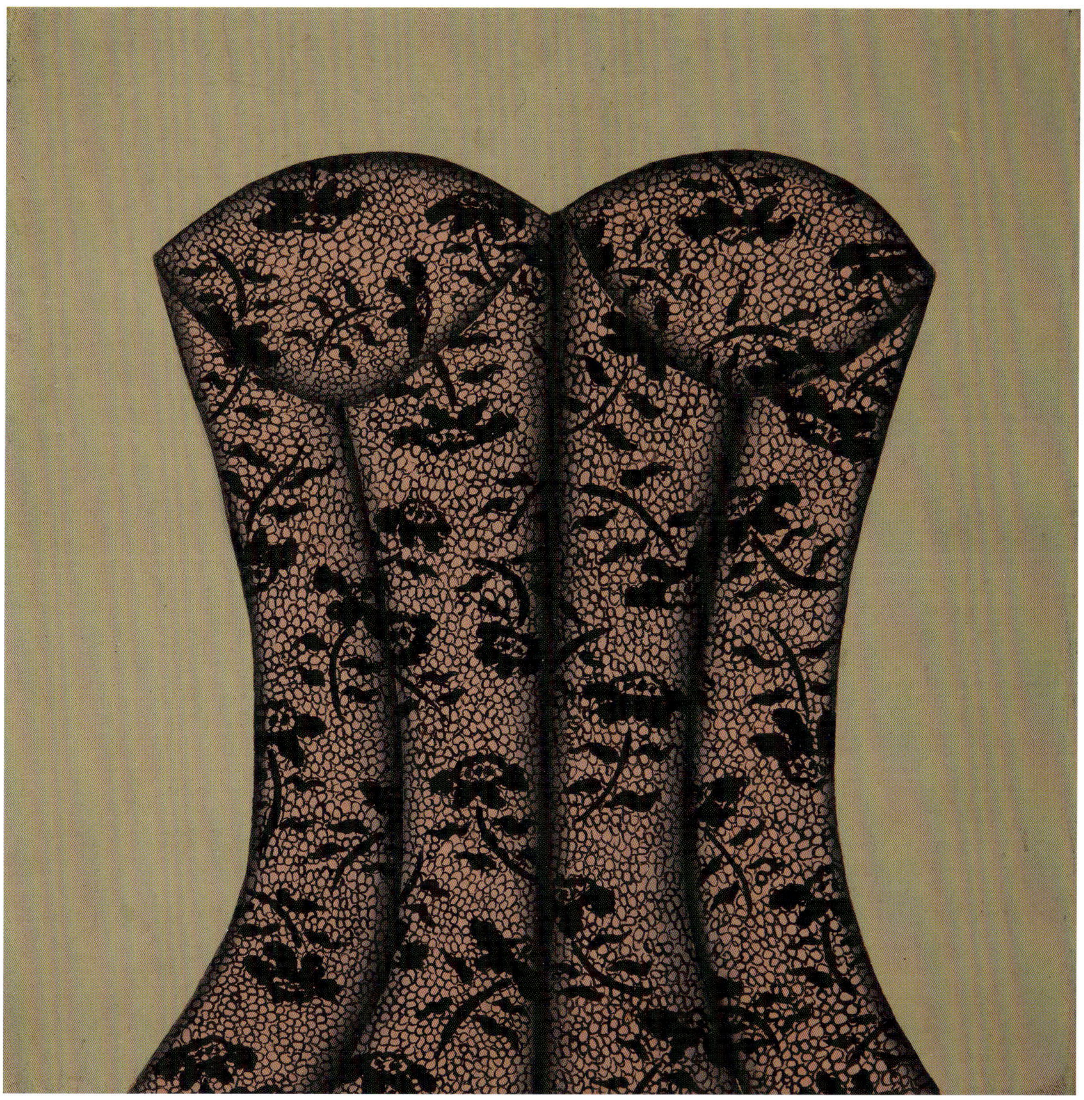

34. *Untitled (Corset)*, 1971
Acrylic on pressed board
Collection of the DePaul Art Museum, gift of funds from the Judith Rothschild Foundation, 2007.27

MARCOS RAYA

Marcos Raya has left his creative fingerprints on Chicago's landscape. A native of Irapuato Guanajuato, Mexico, Raya arrived in the United States as a young man. In his early years as an artist in Chicago, he was one of the chief drivers of the city's Mexican Mural Movement. He is also an accomplished painter and installation artist. Many of Raya's works are filled with political allusions and angry commentaries on societal ills. His in-your-face artistic style compels you to pay attention to his messages. In his best work, Raya reveals his inner worldview, which is full of sad, cold, hypocritical, sinister, hopeless, and politically corrupt images—a world devoid of humanity. In 2010 Raya was featured in a three-man exhibition at the Hospicio Cabañas in Guadalajara, together with the great artistic giants José Clemente Orozco and Fernando Botero.

CARLOS TORTOLERO

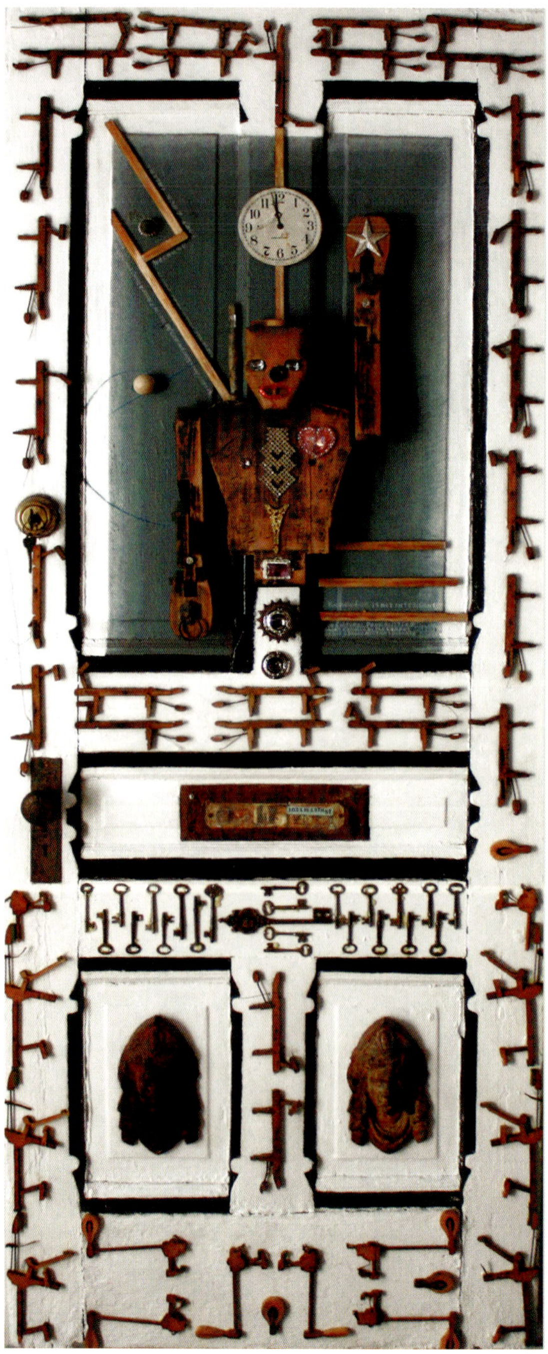

35. *Homage to the Street*, 1997
Mixed media
Collection of the artist

SUELLEN ROCCA

Suellen Rocca is a central figure in the artistic currents that have come to be loosely called Imagism. Many of the artists associated with this development, which emerged in the late 1960s, were students or faculty at the School of the Art Institute of Chicago. While all of the Imagists have highly individual styles, points of view, and subjects, they have in common a pronounced involvement with organic forms, strong color, and complex personal symbols that are figurative in nature. The Imagists share a variety of visual interests and influences, including folk art, art of the insane, outsider art, art of indigenous peoples, advertising and comic-book subjects, medieval and early Renaissance art, Surrealism, and Dada. An appealing aspect of much Chicago Imagism is its concern with wit and satirical references to commercial and popular visual images.

Rocca's 1968 *Dream Girl* explores a world of teenage preoccupations with body image, accessories, and fashion trends. Rocca presented her vision with a dizzying richness of forms and ingenious compositional devices like the divided picture field and the shifting scale of bodily images such as feet, hands, legs, and a large torso in the upper section of the composition. In the top corners are sleeping heads laid on pillows, indicating the importance of dreams as sources of the artist's imagery and subjective concerns. Rocca's inventive employment of this personal content gives her work an affable and good-natured charm despite its occasionally alarming details.

DENNIS ADRIAN

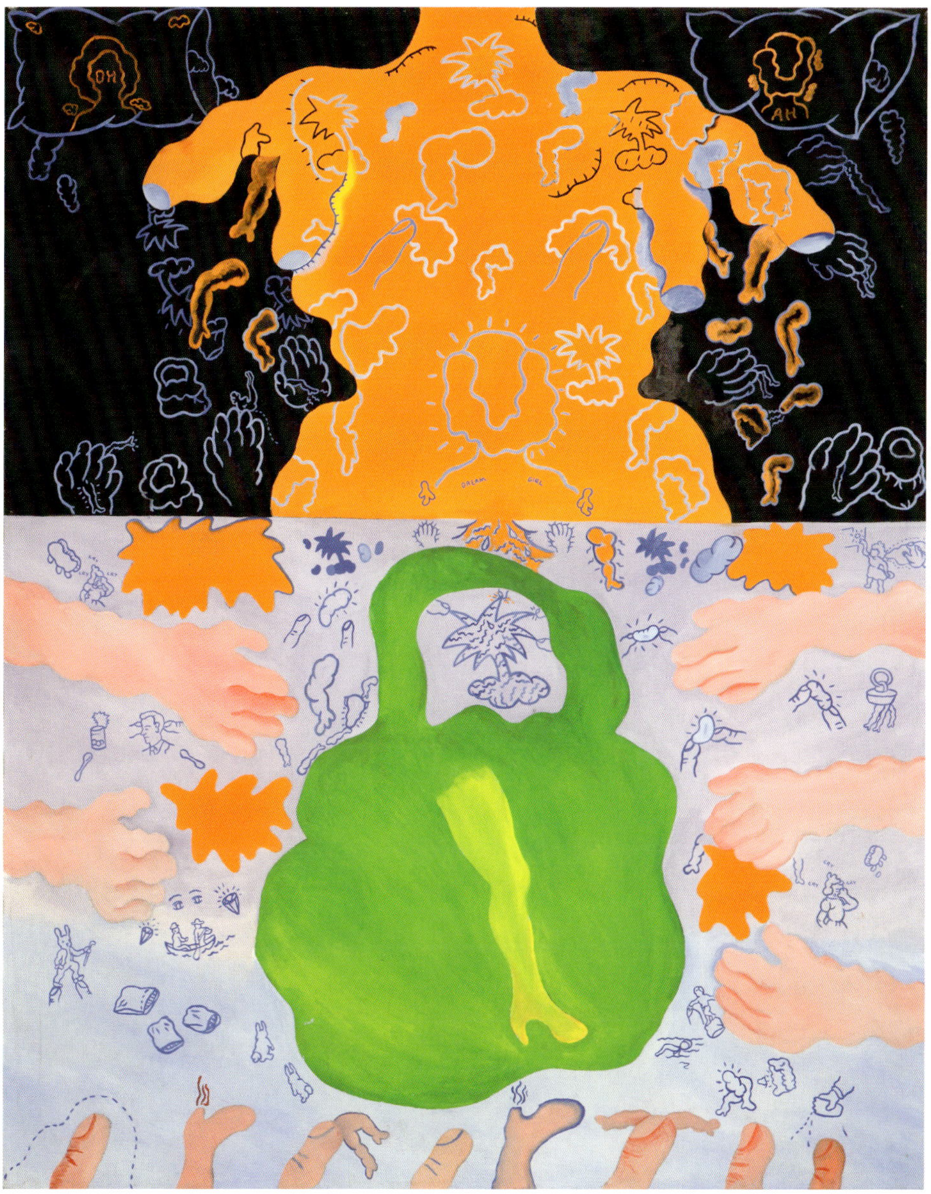

36. *Dream Girl*, c. 1968
Oil on canvas
Collection of the DePaul Art Museum, 2011.6

ART SHAY

Art Shay is one of the several stellar jewels in the crown of Chicago photography. In a richly textured city that invites shooting on the streets and in the saloons, Shay is our sweet home's world-class photojournalist. He practiced in the mid-twentieth century, when photographic freedom blossomed into direct encounters with the world as it is. Having worked for big magazines like *Life*, *Fortune*, and *Sports Illustrated*—and having taken time out for his own forays into the streets—Shay recorded meaningful moments of high and low life with keen discernment and unsparing precision.

Shay reached the perfection of his form in his series on the life of his friend, Chicago's literary lion Nelson Algren. Suffused with a film-noir aesthetic, the series captures Algren in his multifarious moods and haunts, providing insight into and connection with this complex character. Though plans to publish the series in *Life* were never realized, Shay's photographs of Algren have since become a paragon in his prolific career. The visual intelligence and sensitivity that Shay brought to his encounter with Algren informs the entirety of his body of work.

MICHAEL WEINSTEIN

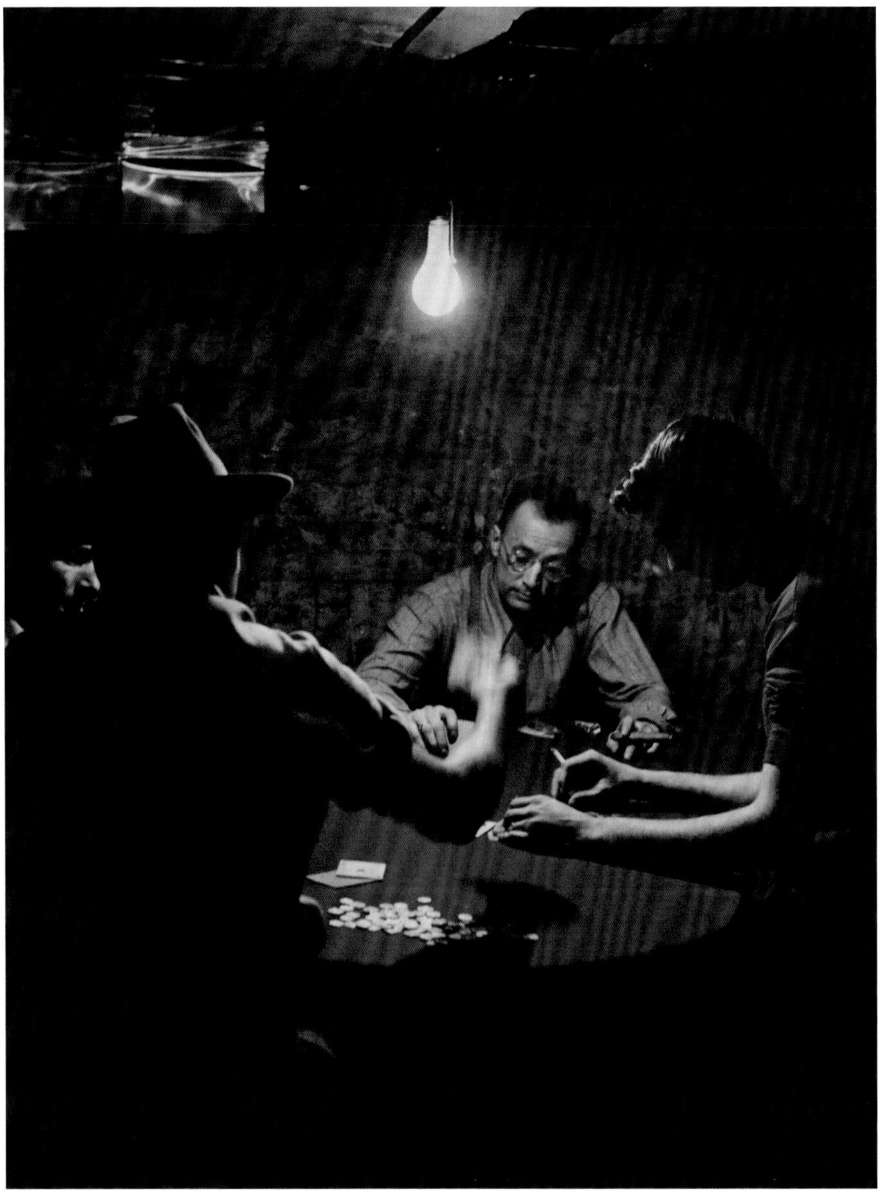

37. *Untitled (Poker Game)*, 1949
Gelatin silver print
Collection of the DePaul Art Museum, gift of Art Shay, 2011.14

LORADO TAFT

Simultaneously linked and isolated around an amorphous mass, the four figures of *The Solitude of the Soul* embody the existential isolation of the individual. Sculptor Lorado Taft and his contemporaries saw impenetrable loneliness as a particular consequence of modern life, notably epitomized by Chicago itself. The spiritual uplift of high art, he argued, was an essential antidote to the social fragmentation, psychic alienation, and spiritual degradation engendered by urbanism, industrialism, and modern mass culture.

The Solitude of the Soul combines the idealized human form, so prized in the classical tradition in which Taft was trained, with an emphatic materiality and expressive modeling influenced by the French sculptor Auguste Rodin. Through these means, Taft sought both to invoke universal ideas and to address contemporary concerns. This bronze cast from his plaster model of 1901 is an early version of a concept best known from the full-size marble rendition commissioned by the Art Institute of Chicago in 1911.

Taft was Chicago's most prominent sculptor in the decades around the turn of the twentieth century. A prolific writer, lecturer, and educator, he was equally influential as a tireless national missionary for art. Taft spoke for many when he opposed what he regarded as the "soullessness" of modernism; for this, and for his conservative adherence to aesthetic idealism, he became a favorite target of Chicago's artistic radicals of the second two decades of the twentieth century.

WENDY GREENHOUSE

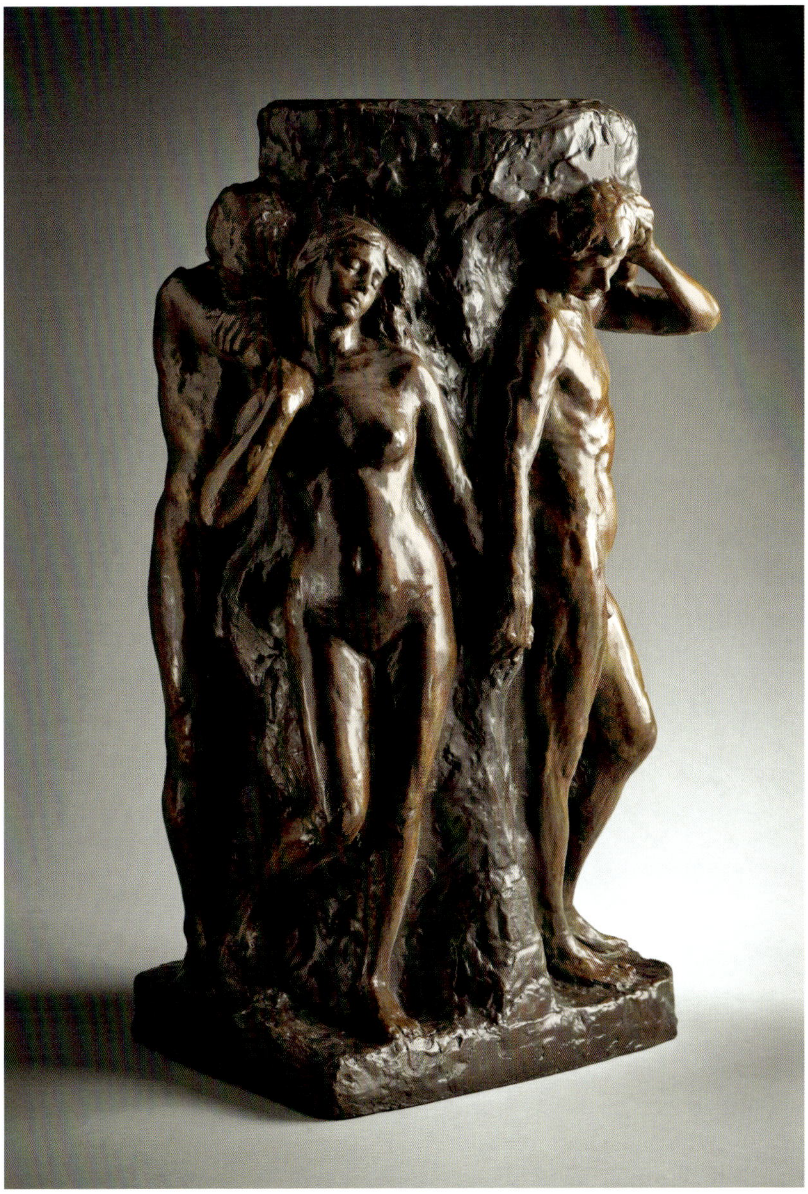

38. *The Solitude of the Soul*, modeled 1901, cast 1944
Bronze
Los Angeles County Museum of Art, purchased with funds provided by the American Art Council, Dr. and Mrs. Robert Carroll, Mr. and Mrs. John M. Liebes, Luppe H. and Kate Luppen in honor of Donald Reed, Brenda, Gary and Harrison Ruttenberg, and Mr. and Mrs. William Lippman, AC1994.133.1

MORRIS TOPCHEVSKY

Morris Topchevsky was a painter who leaned emphatically to the Left. His political views, which formed the basis for his art, arose in part from the oppression of Jews in his native Poland, where four of his siblings died in the Bialystock pogrom of 1906. Topchevsky immigrated to Chicago with his family in 1910, studied at the School of the Art Institute of Chicago, and worked as a billboard painter. He met Jane Addams, the founder of Hull House, a social-service agency on the city's west side. Sharing a concern for the plight of the working class and a belief that art could advance the cause of the underprivileged, Topchevsky and Addams traveled to Mexico in 1925 to observe how local leaders there were working to improve living conditions in impoverished areas. While there Topchevsky met the muralists Diego Rivera and José Clemente Orozco, who further inspired him to use art as a tool for social change.

Topchevsky's *A Century of Progress*, painted around 1933, dramatically illustrates the contrast between the fair's utopian theme of advancement and the sorry reality experienced by ordinary, out-of-work Americans. The gleaming modernist architecture of the fair sits majestically in the background, truly a world apart from the group of homeless men that are the subject of this work.

ROBERT CLIFFORD
(TEXT BY PATTI GILFORD)

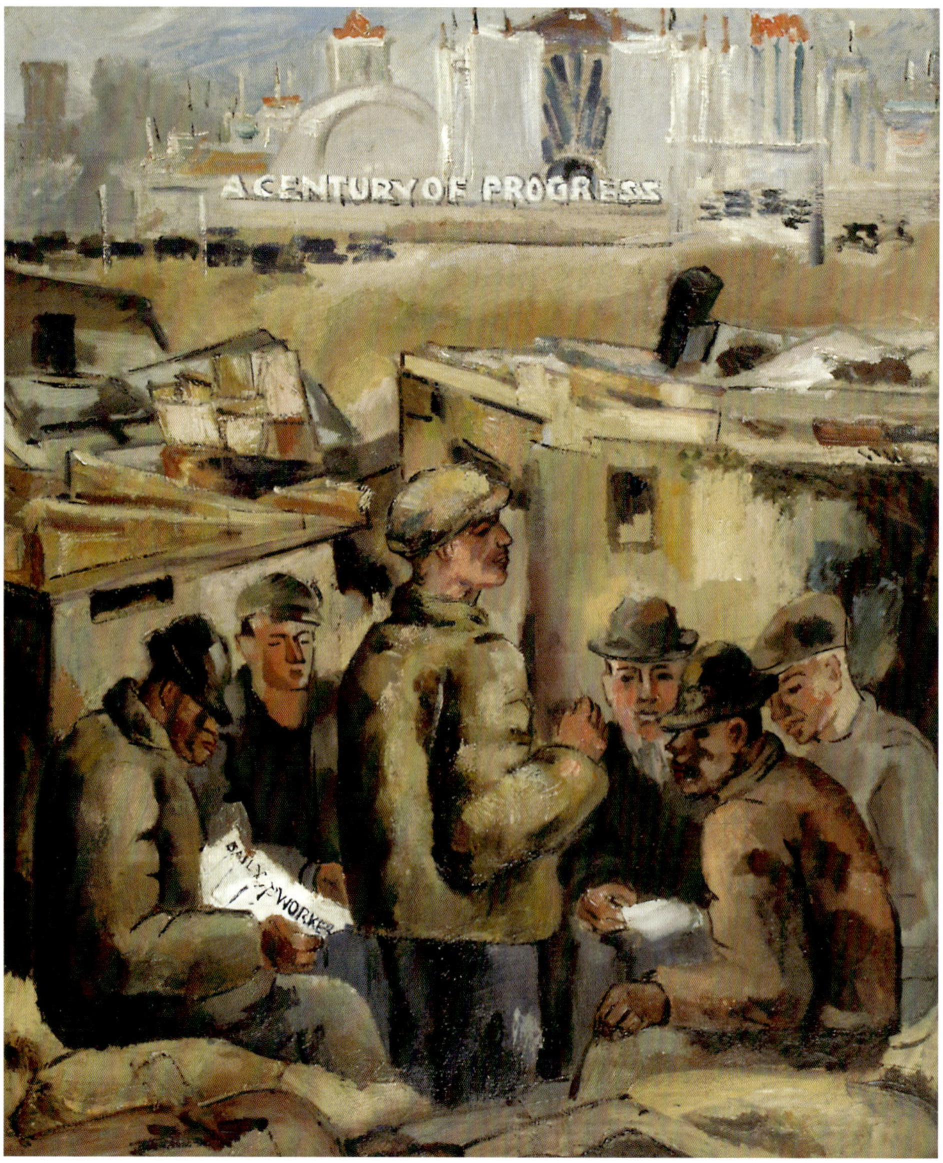

39. *A Century of Progress*, c. 1933
Oil on canvas
Clifford Law Offices, Chicago

OLI WATT

Over the last six years, one thing has become clear to me: Richard Holland and I are never interested in the same artworks. It makes any situation in which we share a recommendation (as representatives of our podcast and blog, *Bad at Sports*) difficult. Strangely, or not so strangely, we both wholeheartedly love the work of Oli Watt. Whether it be the "working-artist" charm of his composition representing Old Style six-pack carriers in a very gray world, his depiction of a single playing card with a value of twenty-one, or his creation of doppelgängers for local hardware-store ephemera, he reminds us that every part of the world is, or can be, worth considering. Well, at least it might be good for a laugh.

With Watt's work, it is often difficult to determine whether or not he is "kidding." He could be just making a joke that feels funny, if ever so slightly fleeting, or maybe he is earnestly offering a poetic and aesthetic suggestion. Such is the case with *No Parking*, which plays with typical Chicago roadwork signage to produce objects that are uncanny and romantic. That might be the beauty latent in a value scale of apparently sun-faded street-cleaning signs. These works seek to remind us to pull back from the serious and overwrought—have a laugh, damn it! Life is pretty amazing, and the banal is just another possible hiding place for joy.

RICHARD HOLLAND AND
DUNCAN MACKENZIE

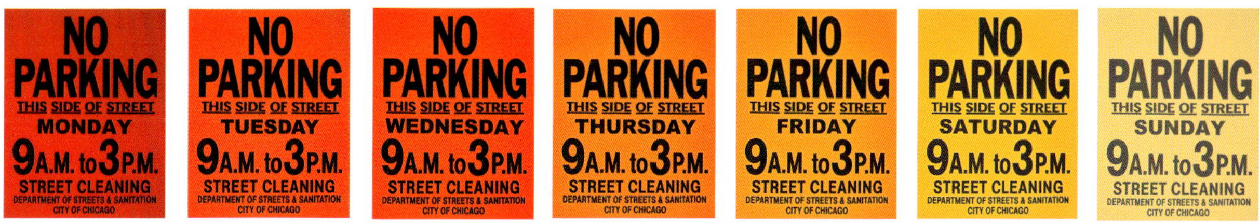

40. *No Parking*, 2007
Screenprint
Collection of the artist

KARL WIRSUM

Some might say that Chicago Imagist Karl Wirsum is a well-established artist with a big reputation, but I believe he is so very good and seems so undervalued, in both the national and international art world and even somewhat in Chicago. Among the Imagists, he seems to have garnered the least international attention, which initiates a story of art politics and the like. Nonetheless, his influence is huge—his work predates by decades the rediscovery of the graphic-novel and pop-culture content so in vogue among younger artists today. For over thirty years, he has worked on developing his own voice, independent of the vagaries of the business of art. Maybe it is time for the art world (power brokers and audience) to catch up to the passion, sincerity, well-crafted beauty, and good-natured fun contained in his ongoing body of work. He is a Chicago treasure, and the rest of the world would be well served to take notice.

LANNY SILVERMAN

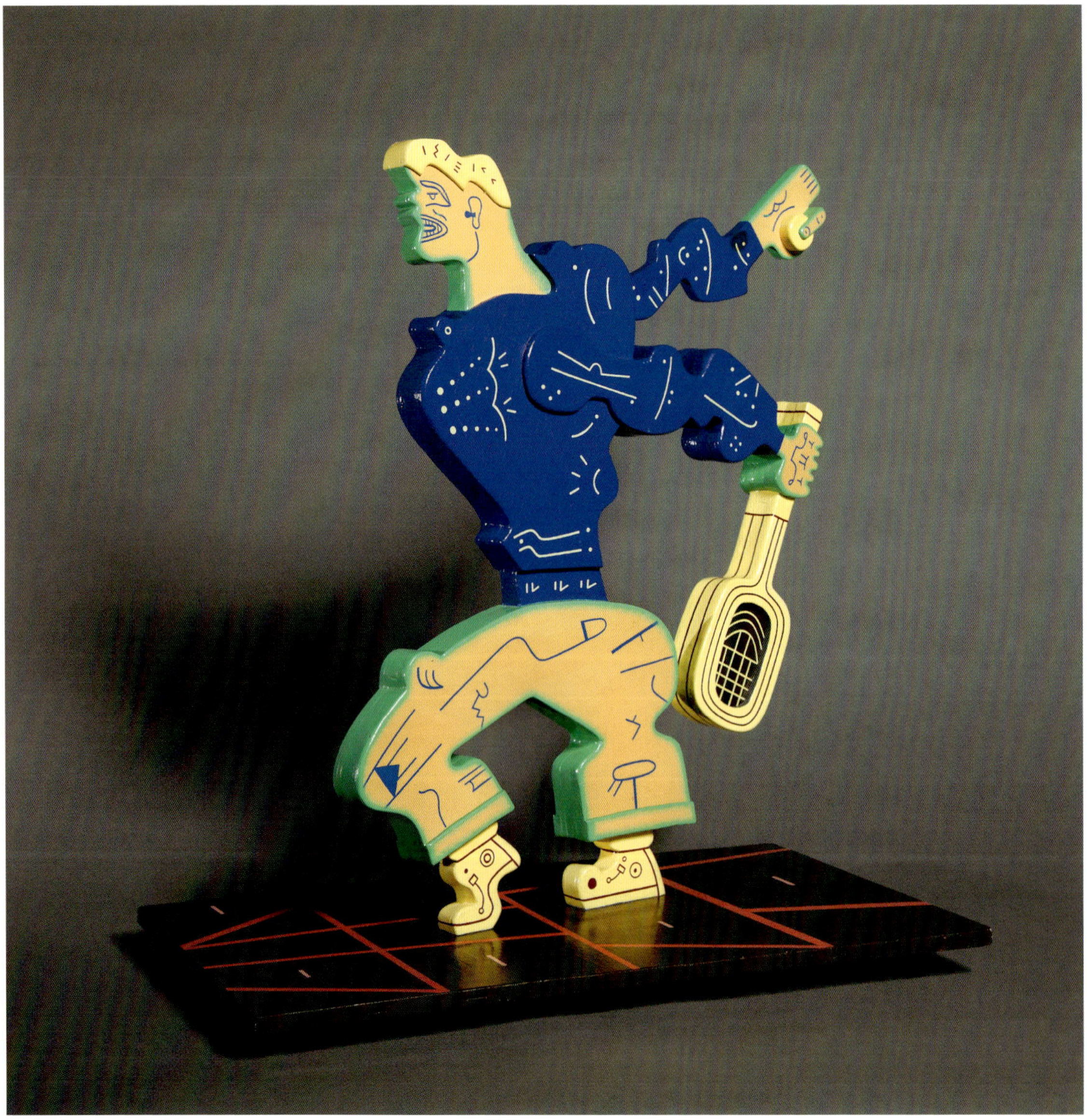

41. *Service Station*, 1979
Acrylic on wood
Collection of the DePaul Art Museum,
Art Acquisition Endowment, 2010.20

RE: CHICAGO EXHIBITION CHECKLIST

Gertrude Abercrombie (American, 1909–1977)
Split Personality, 1954
Oil on pressed board; 8 × 10 in.
Collection of the DePaul Art Museum,
Art Acquisition Endowment, 2010.21

Ivan Albright (American, 1897–1983)
Self-Portrait, 1934
Oil on canvas; 30 1/4 × 18 1/4 in.
New Trier Township High School District 203,
Winnetka, Illinois

Tim Anderson (American, born 1954)
AB-EX, 2008
Oil and graphite on canvas; 34 × 40 in.
Collection of the artist

Ralph Arnold (American, 1928–2006)
Who You/Yeah Baby, c. 1968
Oil and collage on canvas; 30 1/8 × 24 1/4 in.
Collection of the DePaul Art Museum,
Art Acquisition Endowment, 2008.81

Macena Barton (American, 1901–1986)
Self-Portrait, c. 1932
Oil on canvas; 42 × 32 in.
Collection of Mr. and Mrs. Harlan J. Berk

Don Baum (American, 1922–2008)
ARF, 1986
Mixed-media sculpture; 24 × 19 3/4 × 26 in.
Estate of Don Baum, courtesy of
Carl Hammer Gallery

Marie Krane Bergman and Cream Co.
(American, born 1962)
Years, Years Later, in Weeks, 2011
Acrylic on thread, paperclips, and shadows;
dimensions variable
Courtesy of Cream Co.

Dawoud Bey (American, born 1953)
Muhammad (Chicago), 2001
Archival pigment print; 40 × 32 in.
Collection of the DePaul Art Museum,
Art Acquisition Endowment, 2011.13

Margaret Burroughs (American, 1917–2010)
Peace, 1967
Oil on Masonite; 23 1/2 × 17 in.
Collection of Shay and Christopher Brokemond

Harry Callahan (American, 1912–1999)
Untitled, 1960
Gelatin silver print; 8 1/8 × 12 1/16 in.
Collection of the DePaul Art Museum,
Art Acquisition Endowment, 2003.15

Harry Callahan (American, 1912–1999)
Lake Michigan (Eleanor and Barbara), c. 1953
Gelatin silver print; 8 × 10 in.
Collection of Wayne Miller, courtesy of
Stephen Daiter Gallery
(not in catalogue)

Nick Cave (American, born 1959)
Soundsuit, 2010
Mixed media; 101 × 26 × 14 in.
Courtesy of Jack Shainman Gallery, New York

Juan Angel Chavez (American, born Mexico 1971)
No Campground Just Water, c. 2005
Found objects and plywood; 84 × 84 × 84 in.
Collection of the artist

William Conger (American, born 1937)
Gemini (diptych), 1974
Oil on canvas; each panel: 42 1/4 × 33 1/8 in.
Collection of the DePaul Art Museum,
gift of Mary and John Gedo, 2008.76-77

Paul D'Amato (American, born 1956)
634 W. Division, Chicago, 2007
Archival pigment print; 31 × 40 in.
Collection of the DePaul Art Museum,
Art Acquisition Endowment, 2010.69

Henry Darger (American, 1892–1973)
*2 at Cedernine..../15 at Battle of
Norma Catherine*, n.d.
Watercolor and graphite on paper; 11 1/8 × 47 7/8 in.
Collection of Bob Roth

Arthur B. Davies (American, 1862–1926)
Helen, the Dawn Flower, c. 1908
Oil on canvas; 24 × 18 in.
Owen Yost Collection, Florida

Davis/Langlois
Robert Davis (American, born 1970) and
Michael Langlois (American, born 1974)
Living the Dream, 2011
Site-specific mixed-media installation; dimensions variable
Collection of the artists; courtesy of moniquemeloche gallery, Chicago

Manierre Dawson (American, 1887–1969)
Study for Differential Complex, 1910 (?)
Oil on canvas; 16 × 12 1/4 in.
Collection of David and Mary Winton Green, Wilmette, Illinois

Tony Fitzpatrick (American, born 1958)
The Winter Tiger, 2010
Graphite, ink, pigment, and found materials on archival board; 11 3/4 × 8 3/4 in.
Collection of the DePaul Art Museum, Art Acquisition Endowment, 2010.70

Ramon Gabriel (American, born Virgin Islands, 1910–1987)
String Quartet, c. 1945
Watercolor on paper; 7 1/2 × 12 in.
Collection of the DePaul Art Museum, Art Acquisition Endowment, 2010.4

George Healy (American, 1813–1894)
Portrait Bust of a Man, 1865
Oil on canvas; 18 1/8 × 24 3/16 in.
Collection of the Terra Foundation for American Art, gift of Mr. and Mrs. John Estabrook, C1983.5

Carl Hoeckner (American, born Germany, 1883–1972)
Cold Steel, c. 1935
Lithograph on paper; 10 1/2 × 16 in.
Mary and Leigh Block Museum of Art, Northwestern University, 1995.50.24

Shane Huffman (American, born 1977)
I'm Not an Alchemist, but I Do Work in Metals, 2011
Gelatin silver print; 40 × 30 in.
Collection of the DePaul Art Museum, Art Acquisition Endowment, 2011. 10

Richard Hunt (American, born 1935)
Flight Forms, 2002
Steel; 38 × 33 × 33 in.
Collection of Anne and Ed Burke

Richard Hunt (American, born 1935)
Hybrid Form, 1970s
Bronze; 19 × 9 × 5 in.
Collection of Anne and Ed Burke
(not in catalogue)

Margaret Iannelli (American, 1893–1967)
Cover design for *The Fir Tree*, 1916
Ink and graphite on paper; 12 1/2 × 18 in.
Collection of Tim Samuelson

A. Raymond Katz (American, born Hungary, 1895–1974)
The Argument, 1938
Oil on canvas; 58 × 65 in.
Collection of Barry and Merle Gross

Wesley Kimler (American, born 1953)
Five Sisters, 2010
Oil on canvas; 108 × 108 in.
Collection of the artist

Ellen Lanyon (American, born 1926)
The Italian Box, 1973
Oil on canvas; 48 × 36 in.
Collection of the artist; courtesy of Valerie Carberry Gallery

Kerry James Marshall (American, born 1955)
Untitled (Painter), 2010
Acrylic on PVC panel; 47 1/2 × 43 × 4 in.
Collection of Lewis Manilow, Chicago

Archibald Motley (American, 1891–1981)
Knitting Girl, c. 1920
Oil on canvas; 39 1/2 × 29 in.
Bridges Collection, Powell and Barbara Bridges

Gregory Orloff (American, born Russia, 1890–1981)
Paris Pavilion, 1933
Oil on canvas; 27 1/2 × 21 3/4 in.
Collection of Mr. and Mrs. Harlan J. Berk

Angel Otero (American, born Puerto Rico 1981)
Volar, 2011
Collaged oil paint skins on canvas; 72 × 60 in.
Collection of the DePaul Art Museum,
Art Acquisition Endowment, 2011.5

Irving Petlin (American, born 1934)
Untitled, 1955
Oil on canvas; 44 × 35 in.
Collection of the DePaul Art Museum,
Art Acquisition Endowment, 2011.9

Christina Ramberg (American, 1946–1995)
Untitled (Corset), 1971
Acrylic on pressed board; 9 7/8 × 10 in.
Collection of the DePaul Art Museum, gift of funds from the Judith Rothschild Foundation, 2007.27

Christina Ramberg (American, 1946–1995)
Untitled, c. 1969
Acrylic on pressed board; 11 1/2 × 6 in.
Collection of the DePaul Art Museum,
Art Acquisition Endowment, 2006.40
(cover image, not in catalogue)

Marcos Raya (American, born Mexico 1948)
Homage to the Street, 1997
Mixed media; 32 × 83 in.
Collection of the artist

Suellen Rocca (American, born 1943)
Dream Girl, c. 1968
Oil on canvas; 60 × 48 in.
Collection of the DePaul Art Museum, 2011.6

Art Shay (American, born 1922)
Untitled (Poker Game), 1949
Gelatin silver print; 10 × 8 in.
Collection of the DePaul Art Museum,
gift of Art Shay, 2011.14

Art Shay (American, born 1922)
Madison Street on Sunday Morning, 1949
Gelatin silver print; 11 × 14 in.
Collection of the DePaul Art Museum,
Art Acquisition Endowment, 2010.84
(not in catalogue)

Lorado Taft (American, 1860–1936)
The Solitude of the Soul, modeled 1901, cast 1904
Bronze; 29 × 15 × 12 in.
Los Angeles County Museum of Art, purchased with funds provided by the American Art Council, Dr. and Mrs. Robert Carroll, Mr. and Mrs. John M. Liebes, Luppe H. and Kate Luppen in honor of Donald Reed, Brenda, Gary and Harrison Ruttenberg, and Mr. and Mrs. William Lippman, AC1994.133.1

Morris Topchevsky (American, 1899–1947)
A Century of Progress, c. 1933
Oil on canvas; 35 1/2 × 29 1/2 in.
Clifford Law Offices, Chicago

Oli Watt (American, born 1968)
No Parking, 2007
Screenprint; each: 11 × 8 in.
Collection of the artist

Oli Watt (American, born 1968)
Please Turn off the Art, 1998
Engraved sign with light switch; 4 3/4 × 3 in.
Collection of the artist
(not in catalogue)

Oli Watt (American, born 1968)
Proceeding with Caution, 1998
Screenprint; 54 × 36 in.
Collection of the artist
(not in catalogue)

Karl Wirsum (American, born 1939)
Service Station, 1979
Acrylic on wood; 36 × 20 × 34 in.
Collection of the DePaul Art Museum,
Art Acquisition Endowment, 2010.20

NOMINATORS

Carol Adams is President and CEO of the DuSable Museum of African American History in Chicago (*Ramon Gabriel*).

Dennis Adrian is a critic, curator, and art historian who has published extensively on the subject of Chicago art (*Sue Ellen Rocca*).

Harlan J. Berk is an expert in rare coins and a collector of Chicago art (*Gregory Orloff*).

Powell Bridges, an attorney, is a collector of Chicago art from the pre–World War II era (*Archibald Motley*).

Anne Burke is an Illinois Supreme Court Justice and a former trustee of DePaul University. She received a B.A. degree and a Doctor of Humane Letters degree from DePaul University. **Ed Burke** is the alderman of Chicago's 14th Ward. He holds a B.A. degree and a J.D. degree from DePaul University (*Richard Hunt*).

Robert A. Clifford is principal partner of Clifford Law Offices, a collector of Chicago art, and a life trustee of DePaul University. He holds a B.S. degree, a J. D. degree, and a Doctor of Laws degree from DePaul University (*Morris Topchevsky*).

Robert Cozzolino is Curator of Modern Art at the Pennsylvania Academy of the Fine Arts in Philadelphia (*Ivan Albright*).

James Elkins is E. C. Chadbourne Professor of Art History, Theory, and Criticism at the School of the Art Institute of Chicago (*Marie Krane Bergman and Cream Co.*).

Darby English is Associate Professor of Art History at the University of Chicago (*Ralph Arnold*).

Laura Fatemi is the Assistant Director of the DePaul Art Museum (*Tony Fitzpatrick*).

Jason Foumberg is Art Editor and a columnist at Chicago's *Newcity* magazine, writes freelance criticism for *Frieze*, and works at the Art Institute of Chicago (*Nick Cave*).

Mary Gedo is an independent art historian specializing in nineteenth- and twentieth-century art and the author of numerous studies, including *Looking at Art from the Inside Out* (1994) (*Manierre Dawson*).

Matthew Girson is Associate Professor in the Department of Art, Media, and Design at DePaul University (*William Conger*).

Wendy Greenhouse is an independent art historian and curator in Chicago (*Lorado Taft*).

Gregory J. Harris is Assistant Curator at the DePaul Art Museum (*Paul D'Amato*).

Neil Harris is Preston and Sterling Morton Professor of History and of Art History Emeritus at the University of Chicago (*A. Raymond Katz*).

Richard Holland and Duncan MacKenzie are Editor-in-Chief and Executive Producer of *Bad at Sports*, a weekly podcast produced in Chicago about art and the community that makes, reviews, and critiques it (*Oli Watt*).

Joanna Gardner-Huggett is Associate Professor of Art History at DePaul University (*Margaret Burroughs*).

Kirsten M. Jensen is an independent scholar who has published widely on topics in American art, with particular interest in Chicago in the early twentieth century (*Arthur B. Davies*).

Paul Klein is an art critic and Managing Director of the Bridges Group in Chicago (*Wesley Kimler*).

Louise Lincoln is the Director of the DePaul Art Museum (*Don Baum*).

Ed Maldonado is an independent curator based in Chicago (*Angel Otero*).

Lewis Manilow is an attorney, arts patron, and collector of contemporary art (*Kerry James Marshall*).

Ed Marszewski is an arts organizer, founder of the Co-Prosperity Sphere, and publisher of *Proximity* magazine and *Lumpen* (*Juan Angel Chavez*).

Mary Ann Papanek-Miller is an artist and Professor and Chair of the Department of Art, Media, and Design at DePaul University (*Ellen Lanyon*).

Corey Postiglione is an artist, writer, and Associate Professor of Art History and Critical Theory at Columbia College Chicago (*Tim Anderson*).

James Rondeau is Frances and Thomas Dittmer Chair of the Department of Contemporary Art at the Art Institute of Chicago (*Shane Huffman*).

Tim Samuelson is Cultural Historian for the Department of Cultural Affairs of the City of Chicago (*Margaret Iannelli*).

Franz Schulze is Betty Jane Shultz Hollender Professor of Art Emeritus at Lake Forest College (*George Healy*).

Peter Selz is Professor Emeritus in the History of Art Department at the University of California, Berkeley (*Irving Petlin*).

Jamie Shaw is a recent graduate of DePaul University, where she focused on art history and gender studies (*Macena Barton*).

Lanny Silverman was formerly Chief Curator of Exhibitions for the City of Chicago Department of Cultural Affairs (*Karl Wirsum*).

Esther Sparks is Adjunct Assistant Professor of Art History at Valparaiso University and has published extensively on Chicago art (*Carl Hoeckner*).

Carlos Tortolero is the President of the National Museum of Mexican Art in Chicago (*Marcos Raya*).

David Travis is Adjunct Professor of the History of Photography at Columbia College Chicago and former Curator and Chair of the Department of Photography at the Art Institute of Chicago (*Dawoud Bey).*

Mary Trent is Assistant Professor in the Art Department at the University of Wisconsin, Parkside (*Henry Darger*).

Lynne Warren is a curator at the Museum of Contemporary Art Chicago (*Harry Callahan*).

Susan Weininger is Professor Emerita of Art History at Roosevelt University, Chicago (*Gertrude Abercrombie*).

Michael Weinstein is Professor of Political Science at Purdue University and an art critic at Chicago's *Newcity* magazine (*Art Shay*).

Cecile Whiting is Professor and Chair in the Department of Art History at the University of California, Irvine (*Christina Ramberg*).

James Yood is the Director of the New Arts Journalism Program and Adjunct Professor in the Department of Art History, Theory, and Criticism at the School of the Art Institute of Chicago (*Davis/Langlois*).

DePaul Art Museum staff

Louise Lincoln
DIRECTOR

Laura Fatemi
ASSISTANT DIRECTOR

Gregory J. Harris
ASSISTANT CURATOR

Alison Kleiman
ADMINISTRATIVE ASSISTANT

Geoffrey Pettys
ADMINISTRATIVE ASSISTANT

Jenny Cotto
BUILDING MAINTENANCE

INTERNS
Nicole Edwards
Dominic Fortunato
Andrea Jones
Andrew Tripp

This publication was edited by Susan Weidemeyer and designed by Roy Brooks of Fold Four.

Printed by the Fox Company

Photography Credits

All photographs of works of art in the collection of the DePaul Art Museum in this catalogue are © DePaul Art Museum, unless otherwise noted, and photographed by Gregory J. Harris and Dominic Fortunato. All other photography credits are listed below, including material supplied by other institutions, agencies, or individual photographers. Wherever possible, photographs have been credited to the original photographers, regardless of the source of the photograph. All works of art in this catalogue are protected by the express copyright of the individual artists or the artist's estate unless otherwise noted.

Essays

GREENHOUSE
Fig. 1.1: Copyright © Valerie Gerrand Browne; Fig. 1.2: Copyright © Marjorie Albright Lins; Fig. 1.3: Photography © The Art Institute of Chicago; Fig. 1.4: Image courtesy of the University of Illinois Archives; Fig. 1.5: Photography © The Art Institute of Chicago.

JENSEN
Fig. 2.1: Photography © The Art Institute of Chicago; Fig. 2.6: Photography © The Art Institute of Chicago; Fig. 2.7: © Artist Rights Society (ARS), New York / COPY-DAN, Copenhagen.

WARREN
Fig. 3.1: Copyright © Barbara Crane, digital image courtesy of Stephen Daiter Gallery; Fig. 3.2: © 2011 Artists Rights Society (ARS), New York/ VG Bild-Kunst, Bonn; Fig. 3.3: © Aaron Siskind Foundation; Fig. 3.4: Copyright © Kenneth Josephson, courtesy of Higher Pictures, photo © Museum of Contemporary Art Chicago; Fig. 3.5: © Walker Evans Archive, Metropolitan Museum of Art; Fig. 3.6: © Henri Cartier-Bresson, Magnum Photos; Fig. 3.7: Copyright © Yasuhiro Ishimoto, courtesy of Photo Gallery International, Tokyo.

COZZOLINO
Fig. 4.1: © The Art Institute of Chicago; Fig. 4.4: © the Estate of George Paul Thek, courtesy of Alexander and Bonin, New York; Fig, 4.4: Copyright © Peter Saul, courtesy of David Nolan Gallery, photograph by Sandak, Inc., courtesy of the Whitney Museum of American Art, New York; Fig. 4.5: Courtesy of Dominick Di Meo and Corbett vs. Dempsey; Fig. 4.6: Copyright © the Ed Paschke Foundation; Fig 4.9: Copyright © Jim Nutt, courtesy of David Nolan Gallery.

Plates

Cat. 8: Copyright © Dawoud Bey, digital image courtesy of Stephen Daiter Gallery; cat. 10: Copyright © The Estate of Harry Callahan, Courtesy Pace/MacGill Gallery, New York; cat. 11: Photo by James Prinz. Courtesy of the artist and Jack Shainman Gallery, NY; cat. 14: Copyright © Paul D'Amato, digital image courtesy of Stephen Daiter Gallery; cat. 15: Copyright © 2011, Kiyoko Lerner; cat. 21: Digital image courtesy of the Terra Foundation for American Art, Chicago; cat. 25: Copyright © 2011, Scott Elliott; cat. 29: Courtesy of the artist and Jack Shainman Gallery, NY; cat. 30: Copyright © S.P. Bridges; cat. 38: Digital Image © 2009 Museum Associates / LACMA / Art Resource, NY.